GRIEF STALKS

THE

6 O'CLOCK NEWS

by

Barbara Olive

Published by Lemieux International, Ltd.
P.O.Box 170134
Milwaukee, Wisconsin 53217-8011

Some names, places, and incidents have been
changed to protect the confidentiality
of individuals without distorting
the reality of the experience.

ISBN: 0-9667269-7-9

Library of Congress Cataloging-in-Publication Data

Olive, Barbara, Date
    Grief stalks the 6 o'clock news / Barbara Olive.
       p.cm.
    ISBN 0-9667269-7-9 (pbk.)
    1. Grief. 2. Bereavement—Psychological aspects. 3.
Olive, Barbara, 1930- 4. Women—United States—
Biography. I. Title: Grief stalks the six o'clock news.
    II. Title.

BF575.G7 036 2001
155.9'37—dc21
                                        2001046313

This book is dedicated to

Philip and Christopher

who unwittingly shattered

my comfortable world,

and let my soul expand to encompass all

the beauty and wonder of being.

CONTENTS

CONTENTS (continued)

Acknowledgments

First and foremost, I owe profound thanks to my husband, Harry and to our children: Judie, Peter, Mike, Mary, Geri, Cathy, and Peggy. Without their cooperation and support this book would not have been written. Secondly, I want to thank their spouses: Jardo, Sue, Jill, Mike, and Karen for their contributions; I also express a warm and tender thank you to their children who were inadvertently caught up in a drama they did not fully understand till after the story was told.

Many thanks to our acquaintances, friends, relatives, and support groups whose shared grief experiences contributed to our healing and our story. You all know who you are.

I am deeply grateful to my former Lawrence University classmate, Earl Glosser, who gave his expertise and hours of time to reading, critiquing, and contributing the Foreword for this book. Many thanks to Reverend Andre Papineau and to Frances Halpern whose reviews and commentaries have enhanced my efforts.

A special thank you to Judith Janes for her meticulous reading and perfecting of my words, and to my Editor, William Lemieux, who urged me onward during the years it took to complete this book, and whose 'cut, chisel, and polish' editorial skills helped turn it into a compelling narrative.

Foreword

by Earl Glosser

Grief Stalks the 6 O'clock News 'feels' so authentic it's hard to deny that terrible things happen to good people, good families. One can see, hear, and feel what's going on. It's like being there—as if I'm on Olive's shoulder with a TV camera. It's close to a script come alive—'Theatre in the Round'.

Like a stage play there were two grossly different processes at work to get this book into successful production: the creative process, and the 'business' side. The grieving struggle is so long and arduous, yet recovery, to a large extent, is possible. Olive's book gives us *reality* plus *hope*—the best of all messages. This book needs to be read.

The book has obvious appeal for any therapist/clergy person who regularly deals with grief. I'd have every patient/client/group read it—as well as interested friends and family members not directly involved in formal helping efforts. The same could be said about school courses dealing with the topic…a perfect humanizing reading to accompany clinical texts.

People of religious faith will truly enjoy it. They'll feel close enough to feel they've shared with the family, but distant enough to not feel all the pain. They'll accept the multiple reactions couched in her instilled faith languaging that non-church goers will either accept, ignore, or reject

Olive's struggle with Faith ends with it still intact—if not stronger by dint of ordeal. Would anyone write such a book if that had not been the case? I wonder what a Buddhist would have written . . .or a non-believer rational-emotive therapist?

Earl Glosser is Associate Professor Emeritus, University of Virginia, & Founding Director of the University of Virginia Counseling Center.

❧ INTRODUCTION ❧

- You're watching Channel 5 -

For complete in-depth coverage of

Today's Events

Stay tuned for the 6 o'clock report.

*"**Late breaking news: New York,** Death toll from the World Trade Center attack continues to climb. Two more succumb to injuries sustained in the towers' collapse. One woman, a visitor from England, the man, identified as a Trade Center parking attendant."*

*"**California**, Fifteen year old high school student brings gun to school and opens fire on fellow classmates. Two fatally injured, thirteen wounded."*

*"**On the local scene**: Slippery road conditions blamed for seven car pile-up on westbound I-94. Thirty-nine year-old man fatally injured, three others taken to County Emergency Hospital. Two in critical condition, one in satisfactory condition."*

Death on the 6 o'clock news varies in magnitude and intensity. Who can forget the many nights of staring at the Kennedy assassination, the Oklahoma City bombing, and the World Trade Center attack? They are engraved in our memories. Collectively we grieve, pray, perhaps offer help, and assess the impact on our personal space. But what about ordinary daily broadcasts? Can anyone remember a 6 o'clock news report that didn't include at least one traumatic death? A few details, a camera shot, and that's it.

How many tragic announcements do we hear every day during our evening news ritual? How many in a week?… A year?… Let's see. Three per night equals over 1,000 a year. Many report multiple deaths and injuries. . . each sends tentacles of trauma through entire groupings of friends, family, co-workers, and neighbors. Every year we're looking at the involvement of hundreds of thousands of ordinary people.

Death on the Six-o'clock news daily assaults us—a barrage of alarm, horror, intrigue, sadness, shock, pity, and disbelief streams into our emotions, unbalances our nervous systems. Are we a bit bloated at dinnertime? Perhaps irritable during the evening? A touch of insomnia? *Maybe*. Perhaps we laugh off these incidental disasters with the next sitcom. Maybe years of tragic news reports have desensitized our feelings to the daily onslaught.

There is a group of people who cannot laugh them off: the victims, the survivors, and the perpetrators of accidents and violence. Their stories play out for years. Their lives are changed forever. People involved in these 60-second news clips are as traumatized as those we see in history-making headliners. On occasion we are made privy to their ongoing pain, but mostly they remain faceless, forgotten.

The late singer Roy Orbison made one of my favorite observations. His wife divorced him, but within a short time she relented and they were reconciled. Not long after that she was killed in a motorcycle accident. Tragedy struck again when his children died in a fire. Through all this he never stopped performing, traveling, and composing. A friend asked him how he could keep going with all the tragedies in his life. His reply was, "I'm nothing special. You can stop any passerby on the street, and if you ask them the right questions they will have their own tragic story."

We Americans don't take kindly to sharing grief—our own, or particularly others'. We are culturally programmed to remain cool, up-beat, on-top, and self-sufficient. As a result we are a nation of walking wounded. Our grief lies buried under pretense. As a hospital and hospice nurse I heard many tragic stories, and as Orbison says, I have my own story. Like so many others, my family was one of the statistics on the "6 O'clock News".

≫ PROLOGUE ≪

Christopher? In a car accident? In critical condition? I stare dumbly at the telephone receiver clutched in my left hand, my mind puzzling at the words it has just relayed to me.

"Hello. Hello. This is Joanne. Chris has been in an accident. He's in critical condition at County Hospital." Joanne is my son Christopher's mother-in-law.

"Chris?...... My Chris?" Her words refuse to make sense to me.

"Yes." Now I hear the shakiness in her voice. "Here's Karen." Karen is Christopher's wife.

Karen's higher pitched voice comes on choking out words between sobs. "Chris has been in an auto accident. They say he's badly hurt."

"Oh God, no! Not Chris!" In the silence of the darkened living room I feel my throat tighten, my stomach cramp down.

Karen keeps talking rapidly and crying. "I was so worried about him. It kept getting later. He didn't come home. I knew something was wrong. Then the hospital called . . ." her words break off, she is crying too hard to continue.

I hear Joanne's quavering voice again. "We're driving to the hospital now. He's at County Memorial Hospital."

I choke out, "We'll meet you there."

Forcing my hand to move, I replace the phone into its cradle while the words repeat in my ears... becoming real. I can see them now. Stark white letters against black. They start to make pictures. Crushed metal, broken glass, red blood smeared on twisted white flesh.

A pale yellow rectangle of light diffuses through the kitchen doorway from the dim light over the sink, outlining the objects in the living room with gray, fuzzy shadows. I see corners of the end table where the phone rests, my hand still on it, the arm of the couch over which I'm reaching, the caned wooden rocker a few feet away, TV across the room. All in order. All the same. But all is not the same. I am not. Christopher is not.

I remain sitting on the couch, a frightening sense of dread filling me, pushing down on my heart. I know it's time to move, to follow through with the actions required of me. With great effort I rise; my body feels heavy and immobile. I walk back to my bedroom, bracing myself with one hand against the wall, sink down onto my bed and bury my face in my pillow. "Please God," I pray, "Please, no. I don't want to do this again."

My thoughts fall back to a day fourteen months earlier. A tall stranger appeared at my front door to solemnly pronounce the words: "Philip is dead." Philip, my firstborn son, gone. Fresh pain from that loss crushes in on me. I can't go on.

But wait! Christopher is not dead. He's only injured. I've got to keep going. He'll need me now.

⫸ 1 ⫷

Warnings

Warning signs had been popping up for years but I didn't see them. I'm not a person who looks for danger signposts along life's highway—programmed to see partly sunny and ignore partly cloudy. The first alert that breaks through my cultural barrier comes one summer during our annual family campout.

We gather at Point Beach State Park, the place where camping started for Harry and me and our first child, five-year old Judie. Then we rented a nine by nine canvas tent because we weren't sure we'd like grubbing around in the forest. This year we spill over into five campsites with our nine children, five spouses, two friends, and Penny, the family dog. The central campsite is still the one where Harry and I pitch our tent. It's here the cooking is done for the main meal in large blackened soup pots and a massive twenty-four inch diameter frying pan.

By the second day at camp I can't help noticing that our oldest son, Philip, always has a beer in his hand. Neither can I help but notice his flippant replies when I attempt to talk with him. "He's not really drunk," I think, "just acting kind of silly." But then I reason, it's hot out here, it's vacation, and we're all drinking beer and acting silly.

One night I stay up later than usual, sitting on a picnic bench, feeling mellow. I stare into the campfire watching the sparks shoot up into the black sky. Flames hiss and crackle as they discover a pocket of moisture or a trickle of resin. Harry and most of the others have already crawled into their tents for the night. Our children, Philip, Chris, and Mary come over to join me and we talk and joke quietly so as not to awaken the others.

When Philip glances my way I'm startled to see the firelight illuminate a vacuous glassy sheen in his eyes. Is it the dancing fire that lights them so strangely? I study the faces of Chris and Mary. Even with the firelight reflecting in their eyes, they look calm and focused. I try to assess Philip's sobriety by engaging him in conversation. He doesn't turn to look at me, he doesn't even seem to hear me. I realize that he never looks me in the eye anymore, never seems willing to share his thoughts with me— certainly not during this camping trip. "He keeps making a joke about everything," I think uneasily.

As he pokes at the fire stirring up the coals he begins singing long funny verses of Burl Ives' "Gray Goose". We laugh at first enjoying the nonsense rhymes, but they go on and on. He chuckles to himself and seems to be out of touch with the rest of us. First Mary, and then Chris excuse themselves and go off to bed. I sit there for a while watching Phil, feeling very sad. I love him. I wish he would talk to me. Later, cocooned in my sleeping bag, I talk to God about this phantom stranger who is supposed to be my son.

One of his brothers detects something amiss. We're home from camp a few days when I get a mid-week call from Peter in Boston. We usually call to chat on weekends when rates are lower, so I know he has something special in mind. "Hi, Peter. What's up?"

"I'm kind of worried about Phil, Ma. He called me late last night, rambled on about a lot of stuff that didn't make any sense. I made out a couple of sentences. Something about Dad drinking too much and it's all his fault. He went on talking but that's all I could figure out. I don't know. Maybe you should check on him and see if he's okay."

"I'd better give him a call. I've been worried about him myself. Did you notice how much he was drinking at camp? How he seemed kind of detached from the rest of us?"

"I saw him tossing down a lot of brew. 'Course, I wasn't doing so bad myself. But Phil, well, he looked pretty loaded at times."

"I'm glad you called Peter. I'll call Phil in the morning and see how he's doing."

I get Philip on the phone at lunch time the next day. "Haven't seen you since our camping trip, Phil. How's everything going?"

"Pretty good." His voice, sounding flat and dull, tells me he isn't doing all that good. "I'm putting in hours of work on this addition to the house. I'll be glad when it's done. I'm getting pretty sick of it." I squirm in my chair wondering how I can bring up his drinking problem without hurting his feelings. I've always hated confrontations like this and avoid them whenever possible. While Philip is speaking, I figure out how to work alcohol into the conversation.

"Peter called last night. He told me he's worried about you."

"What's he worried about me for?"

"Well, he noticed you were drinking a lot more beer this summer. Then when you called him last night he thought you sounded like you had a few too many."

"I have been going pretty heavy on the beer, Mom. But don't worry. I'm cutting back. The trouble was with that volunteer fire department I belonged to. I sat around the station with the rest of the guys drinking beer by the gallon. I've dropped out of that. I'll be better off."

"I'm glad you're cutting down. Peter's not the only one concerned about you. I couldn't help noticing you were drinking more than usual at camp. To tell the truth, I've been worried too."

"No problem, Mom."

"That's good to hear. You take care of yourself now. Stop in to see us when you're in town." Satisfied that Phil has his drinking under control, I dismiss the problem—except during prayer time, when I ask for God's blessing on each of our children. Very soon a new project crowds in to fill my thoughts.

In the beginning the investment idea is Peter's. "Ma, the property around the University is a great bargain. We could go halves on a house there. Maybe get Mike to manage it so it won't be much work for you." Peter's new Master's Degree is paying off with a bigger salary and he wants a deal that will make his savings grow.

He's right about the great bargain. I watched the price of houses edge up on Milwaukee's East Side ever since the university began expanding its campus there fifteen years ago. Apartments and duplexes were in great demand to house students, and larger houses were sought out by professors and assorted intelligentsia. It had become a much sought after section of real estate. Along with the posh estates bordering Lake Michigan, the East Side was becoming Milwaukee's new 'Gold Coast'.

I pour over Real Estate ads to find the ideal bargain house, and drive through Eastside streets to hunt down 'For Sale' signs and call the agents who posted them.

About a month later Sue calls. "We finally finished the new addition to our house and we're having a party to celebrate." They live in a small caretaker's cottage on the grounds of a religious retreat house where Philip is in charge of building and ground maintenance. Their two children, Josh and Sarah, are now too old to share the same bedroom, so they added on an extra bedroom and more living space. The religious order graciously put up money for the project. Phil did most of the work himself. "We want all of you to see how beautiful the new rooms turned out. Phil did a wonderful job," Sue adds.

The party Sunday arrives and Sue starts the festivities by giving us a tour of the new rooms. She is especially excited about the sewing room Philip has designed for her inside a large walk-in closet. "Where is Phil?" I ask, surprised that he isn't showing off his own handiwork.

Sue glances at me, then quickly looks away pressing her lips together. I see she wants to say something but won't let the words come out. I don't want to question her in front of the others. We sit down to enjoy refreshments and chat.

Half an hour goes by before Philip enters the house. His feet are bare. He's wearing stained jeans and a wrinkled flannel shirt. It's obvious he hasn't combed his hair for some time. He has a gaunt, crumpled appearance, with dark half-circles under his eyes.

I approach him to say hello, fighting to suppress my annoyance that he hasn't cleaned up for the party. He says little more than "Hello" and makes no apologies for his appearance. He doesn't say much while the rest of us enjoy the buffet supper Sue prepared. He picks at the food on his plate.

Sue takes me aside while we're cleaning up the dishes and begins filling me in on the painful facts behind Philip's appearance. "He's been drinking too much for a long time. I know he has at least a six pack of beer a day, maybe more."

"I thought he was drinking a lot at camp this summer, but I talked to him about a month ago. He told me he had everything under control."

"I'm afraid not. Things have gotten way out of hand. He's started having periods of time where he can't remember anything. A few days ago he broke down, crying uncontrollably for hours. Said he didn't know why." We absently rub towels over the wet dishes, and Sue stacks the dry ones in the cupboards.

"Sue, why didn't you tell me about this? Maybe I could have talked to him or helped in some way." I hear my voice rising in volume and pitch and strive to keep it under control.

"I didn't want to worry you. You've got so much on your mind already. I had a long talk with Father Tom." Father Tom manages the retreat house and is an old friend of Harry's family. He's the priest who performed Phil and Sue's wedding ceremony eleven years ago. "Between us we've gotten Phil to agree to go in for therapy for his alcoholism." The 'a' word sends a jolt through me and I grab the edge of the sink to steady myself. It's the first time I connect alcoholism with Philip. "He's leaving for inpatient treatment tomorrow. His doctor says he'll be there at least a month, maybe two or three."

Her words feel like a physical blow. "Oh my God! I had no idea things were this bad. He never tells me anything."

Having decided to get the whole story out, Sue pushes on. "Father Tom arranged for Phil to take a leave of absence from his caretaking duties. He's hired a boy to take care of the retreat house and grounds."

"You'll be all alone here with Josh and Sarah." Josh was nine and Sarah only seven. "Who's going to take care of them while you're at work? Doesn't Phil usually take care of them when you're away?"

"They'll be in school most of the time and a neighbor has agreed to watch them till I get home from work." Her forehead wrinkles up in a worried look. "This is going to be really hard on me, though. I'm trying to get through that Master's in Social Welfare this semester. I've got so much studying to do." Her eyes look desperate as they search mine for help.

"Harry is home all the time now that he's retired. He can help watch the kids. I can help on my days off."

"That's good. I might need both of you. I'm not sure how this is going to work out." We hang our dish towels over the back of the oven to dry, and struggle to compose ourselves before going back to the other guests.

On a gray Sunday afternoon in October, Philip, Josh, Sarah, and I shuffle slowly along the paved walks encircling the inpatient clinic. Josh and Sarah kick at the colored leaves that have fallen from the old elms and maples growing in abundance on the grounds. The grass, hanging on to a tinge of fresh green color, is restful to our eyes; the air is still and quiet. "This seems like a peaceful, healing place."

"It is," Philip nods. "It's good to be free from the usual worries about work and the kids. This is like being in a separate world from everyone else. I have lots of free time to think. I sure do miss the kids, though. It's good of you to bring them." This is the first time in months he's communicating his thoughts to me.

"I was happy to bring them. I thought Sue could use the afternoon off to study. Besides, we all miss you."

"You do?" He looks at me in surprise. "Well, I miss you too." We stop walking to wait for Josh and Sarah who are pushing the dry leaves into a pile next to the walk. "I'm glad you're looking out for Sue. I feel kind of helpless right now, cut off from her and the kids. All this extra responsibility is hard on her."

"Everybody's pitching in to help. Your job now is to take care of yourself." We smile at the kids as they take flying leaps into their hill of leaves.

"You're right. This is good for a while, to be free of all those pressures life dumps on me... I've been taking care of others for so long I forgot what I needed." My eyes follow his as they sweep over the rambling, unobtrusive buildings. "Nothing to do here but pray, meditate, and take part in the counseling sessions."

"Sounds good to me." I take a deep breath of the moist, woodsy air and feel my body relaxing. "Maybe we all need this once in a while."

"We do. I needed it a lot. I'm glad I came in

when I did. I'm still in good shape. You should see some of the guys they bring in here. They carried a couple of them in on stretchers. Their bodies are shot, their minds too. That's the way I would have been if I kept on drinking."

I'm grateful he's speaking honestly about how he feels. I'm getting to talk to the *real* Philip again. It's a good afternoon.

It takes three months of intensive inpatient treatment for Philip to overcome his excessive drinking. By then he knows he can never take another drink without slipping back into alcoholism. His therapist discovers that his root problem is the severe depression that lured him into the habit of drinking. This proves to be the toughest symptom to cure.

For two years Philip continues weekly sessions of both private and group therapy. His doctor experiments with different anti-depressants in varying doses. In my interactions with him during these years, he's an empty shell. Feeling, enthusiasm, and joy have been sucked out. Dull and solemn, he sometimes gives me a reason for his unhappiness.

"We almost got a good piece of farmland at a reasonable price but when we were ready to sign the contract the lady backed down on the deal." He's wanted his own farm since he graduated from high school.

Then there is an unsettling remark about trouble in his relationship. "Sue is paying more attention to her career than to our marriage." My better instincts tell me never to interfere in my children's marriages. As the weeks drag on I wonder—should I inquire more deeply into their problems?

Philip's glum spirits are picked up by the rest of the family. Sue complains, "I'm getting depressed having him moping around the house like this. I can tell it's bothering the kids too. We're all smothering under this blanket of gloom."

After one of these sad encounters with Phil, our daughter Geri startles me with the statement, "I understand what Phil is going through. I felt depressed all the time in high school, even as far back as sixth grade. I know how much he's hurting."

"Geri! I had no idea. You never said anything."

"I know. It felt like something I had to hide. And I didn't want to worry you. Besides," she releases a small contented sigh, "I'm over that awful stage now. When I think back on it I don't know how I could even bear to be alive."

"But when? . . . How did you get over this?" I ask in confusion.

"It happened right after I finished high school. I was working at that grocery store, and, I don't know . . it seemed that one day something just zapped my mind. I began to notice things that made me feel good. Little things like how beautiful that purple plant hanging in the corner of my room was, how good the fabric softener in my pillow smelled . .

. the neat patterns of footsteps in the snow on our front lawn. Then there were big things too, like what a great family I had; how much I love all of you. Gradually, I realized how wonderful it was to be alive. Later, I thought the whole thing was just part of growing up."

While she's speaking I fish a tissue out of my pocket to wipe my flooding eyes. "That's beautiful, that's amazing. I'm so glad you're happy now."

"I hope that's what happens to Philip," she says returning my hug. "I hope something zaps his mind soon. It hurts me to think how miserable he must be."

"Maybe you could tell Phil about your experience. Maybe it would help him."

"I'll try. The trouble is, during the time I was depressed I believed I was a unique case of misery. If someone had told me that I would one day experience a sudden healing and become happy, I wouldn't have believed them. I felt alone . . . and different."

Sometimes, during family parties, we cajole Philip into laughter during a game of cribbage, Trivial Pursuit, or the outdoor antics of a no-holds-barred volleyball game. And there are the deer hunting weekends in November with Harry, Judie's husband Jardo, Philip's friend Frank, Chris and his buddy Matt. Troubles slough away as the boys tramp side by side through the brush, and later sit around the wood stove sharing their deepest feelings.

Through those difficult years I pour out my prayers for Philip daily. Not for a second do I doubt God will eventually heal him. I pray it will be soon. When I feel weighted down with the burden of

Philip's depression, God reminds me He loves Philip more than I do and is guiding him with great tenderness.

❧ 2 ❦

Side Trips

My house-hunting pays off with the best real estate deal available in the East Side neighborhood—a large half-century old, single family house with five bedrooms. Just two blocks from the university campus, it's an ideal location for our children who are completing college courses there. A fastidious German grandmother, no longer able to keep up the house for herself and her handicapped husband, is forced to sell. She's kept the house in good repair, and it's cleaner than most I'd looked at. Inspecting the spacious yard I know that her budding flower beds will be gorgeous in full summer bloom.

The only thing I don't like is the condition of the siding around the lower half of the exterior. Some of the boards will need replacing and the whole section will have to be repainted. The ugly siding is probably what kept the price low. I figure we can live with it—maybe replace it with aluminum siding at a later date.

I call Boston. "I found it, Peter, You're going to love it. It's a sturdy old Victorian with a thick concrete foundation, solid oak floors and woodwork, real lath and plaster walls, and a slate roof that will be intact when the house collapses."

"How much is it going for?"

"Only sixty-five thousand. Cheapest one I've found so far. The lady's anxious to sell so I'm going to offer sixty-three. I can't wait for you to see it. It's got huge windows, some with leaded glass, and this big front hall with an open staircase to the second floor. Halfway up the staircase there's a door that leads to stairs going down to the kitchen at the back of the house. It's really neat. The kitchen looks like it was remodeled in the seventies..."

"Sounds okay, Ma," he says interrupting my patter. "Did you check it out good? Make sure there are no cracks in the foundation? Check out the plumbing, electricity and stuff?" I sense Peter's uneasiness at being so far away and leaving the decisions up to my judgment.

"I had Philip's friend Tom, a building contractor, check it out. He made some suggestions about raising the ground level at two of the corners where rain water might leak in, but says the foundation looks solid. Some electrical wiring could be updated but I figure we can invest a little in that."

Peter's voice sounds more relaxed when he replies. "I suppose we can do that. Well, if Tom says it's okay we might as well jump into the market. I see mortgage rates are low so it's a good time to buy. Sure wish I could be there to help you close the deal."

"I wish you could too, but don't worry. If I have any questions I'll call you right away."

Contracts and specs go back and forth through the mail. On the first of June, Harry goes with me to close. We suddenly have a plethora of prospective tenants anxious to occupy the five bedrooms. Mike, Geri, and Cathy move in immediately. Peggy and her roommate, Janet, plan to move in September 1st when their apartment lease expires.

The four girls pick out bedrooms on the second floor and are content with them without much redecorating. Mike, however, scornfully refers to his bedroom, on one end of the five hundred square feet of attic space, as 'the block room'. In his artistic imaginings he knocks out bedroom walls, elevates the floor two feet above its present level with patio doors opening onto the porch/fire escape we are ordered by law to provide. He plans to insulate the ceiling and walls in the remaining attic space for use as his painting studio/living quarters.

Putting his architectural drawing course to good use, he works up a number of sketches. "I've decided to go with this one," he says in mid-June, holding up front and lateral views of his plan. Some show finished rooms, others the rough framing out and electrical wiring underneath. They hearken back to my nursing school days when we peeled back the skin of anatomical transparencies to reveal muscle, arteries and veins, then other nasty looking parts, at last getting to the skeletal structure which held the whole thing up.

At first I'm impressed. The layout looks like a grandiose scheme from 'Better Homes and Gardens'. Then I feel a nervous twitch in my stomach. Mike has a knack for carpentry and I'm confident in his ability to do the work. But I can see from his plans, that even with him doing most of the labor, this is going to cost us bigtime. Not wishing to dash his hopes I venture timidly, "This is beautiful, Mike, but I'll bet it's going to run into a couple of thousand dollars."

"Well, yeah. Maybe a little more," he says noncommittally. With a good deal of misgiving I agree to the plan. I figure we can always put a stop to the construction if we run out of money.

Before the last can of sealer is applied to the woodwork and the wool Berber carpeting is laid on the elevated bedroom floor, the remodeling project costs us an extra four grand. I have to admit, though, it's a very classy studio bedroom.

On Mike's part the project costs countless hours of hard labor in the stuffy, steamy attic. Throughout the summer I spend most of my spare time holding boards while he saws and hammers at them. His brother Chris does some carpentry, while his wife Karen paints wallboard. Mike enlists the help of his current girlfriend and several of his old school chums whenever possible.

The biggest single helper is Philip. After remodeling his own house, Philip knows what he's doing. Through much of the summer I watch him working alongside Mike. His slim ascetic features, blond wispy hair and blue eyes contrast with Mike's dark Bohemian good looks. I notice that while Phil works with Mike, his patient meditative disposition keeps Mike's temper from flaring over a bent nail or a sliver lodged in a finger. I like having Philip working here. While Mike's intensity charges the molecules around us with frenetic energy, Phil's presence calms them like the silvery quiet of a moonlit sky.

Hearing them joke and laugh I'm relieved that Philip has come back to life. "I sawed this board three times and it's still too short," he says, making a joke about a two-by-four that won't fit into its crevice. At last his depression is lifting. He talks enthusiastically about courses he has signed up for at the university. He's already earned forty-two credits in Chemistry and Agriculture over the past ten years, going part time while working to provide for his family.

Mike has just completed his first year in the Fine Arts Program. He worked for a law firm as a Private Detective; then tried his hand at auto mechanics. Now he's turned in his gun and wrench for his first love, a paintbrush. Bereft of any ability with spatial concepts myself, I am awed watching the continual flow of his creative imagination shaping materials into paintings and sculptures.

"Here's a good one," he says one day picking up a sodden, smashed leather glove from our driveway. "I'm saving these," he says by way of explanation as he hangs it over the back of a chair to dry.

"What on earth for?"

"I'm going to work them into an art piece. If you

run across any save them for me."

"What kind of an art piece?"

"I don't know yet, I'm thinking about it." From that day on I'm keeping my eye out for dead gloves lying in the road.

"Tell me, Harry, where on earth is Lily?" I ask bending over a map of Wisconsin I have spread open on the coffee table. With so much of the family's time being invested in the new attic, we decide to skip our annual family camping trip. Some of us take side trips when we can get away. Harry and I decide to drive to Brookston, Minnesota to visit our daughter Mary, her husband Mike and their daughter Carli. On the way Harry wants to spend some time with his Uncle Moe who has recently bought a retirement home in Lily, Wisconsin.

"It's near the Wolf River, about fifty miles north of Keshena." The name Keshena floods me with warm and frantic memories of visits to my parents' home on the Menominee Indian Reservation. Our brown Clubwagon was stuffed with suitcases, sleeping bags, nine children (plus a friend or two), and our old Shelty dog, Penny. I can still see the apprehensive look on mother's face as she stood on her back porch and watched the van door slide open to emit its swarming contents onto her driveway.

I find the dot on the map with the tiny letters that spell 'Lily'. I judge the distance from Mom's old home on Round Lake at about twenty-five miles.

"Can we stop and see the old place at Round Lake?" After Dad died, Mom sold the lake house and moved back to Milwaukee. We haven't seen it in ten years.

"Sure, we can swing by that way." We plan a leisurely trip to Mary and Mike's, taking in the sights of northern Wisconsin along the way. Mike's job as a warehouse manager requires him to move every couple of years, so it's fun seeing their new house every time we visit them.

The first day we relax and brush up on family news. They treat us to a tour of Duluth, a sparkling clean city, and to beautiful Lake Superior Harbor. I'm teary eyed, as usual, when we say our goodbye's and head for home.

A few days after we unpack our suitcases and settle down to real life, Christopher calls. "I wanted to say goodbye to you and Dad. Karen and I decided to drive out West to see Yosemite, Mount Rushmore and all that good scenic stuff. Neither of us have ever been out West."

"I envy you. Dad traveled out West when he was in the Marines but I've never been west of Minnesota. How long will you be gone?"

"About two weeks. We want to take our time; be able to stop and see whatever grabs us."

We haven't seen much of Christopher since the weather got warm. He's been spending a lot of weekends with Karen's family at their summer house on the Mississippi, boating, fishing, and water skiing—a new thrill for him. He says he's not very good at it.

"He loves to wipe out and crash into the water,"

Karen told us at the beginning of summer. "He says it isn't any fun if you don't fall off."

"That sounds like our Chris," I laugh.

Exciting news comes with the next phone call. Our daughter Judie tells us she and Jardo are taking their family to Disneyworld. "I've wanted to go there all my life," she says calling from Prairie Creek. I can hear the smile in her voice. They've been saving up for the trip for a long time and buy a new Dodge Caravan for the drive. As an impressionable six-year old, Judie turned on the TV one Sunday night to watch Disney's spectacular show and she's been longing to see 'the wonderful world' ever since.

For years Harry and I promised we would take her; even had a jar to collect spare change to pay for it. But instead of trips we had babies, and the coins never once reached the top of the jar. We're thrilled she can take her own family on her dream vacation.

They haven't been gone more than a week when Sue stops in to see us on her lunch hour. With a Social Work Masters on her resume she's snagged a good starter job in Milwaukee not too far from us. She smiles broadly as she says, "I wanted to make sure you know that Phil and I are planning a trip to Boston this month. I didn't know if Phil said anything to you."

"That's wonderful, Sue. He didn't tell us. Are you going to stay with Peter and Jill?"

"Part of the time. We've got friends out East we want to visit too."

"That's so great. You're going to love Boston.

And you and Phil haven't gone anywhere except camping for years."

"I know. I'm glad Phil agreed to go. He hates to travel. But this summer, he seems willing to do more. He seems much happier than he's been for years."

"That's what I thought too. Since he started helping Mike in our attic, they're always laughing and joking. We've all been worried about him, about you too, but it looks like he's finally gotten over his depression."

"I guess you don't have to worry anymore." A pleased smile slowly spreads across her face. "He's definitely in a better mood." Her smile turns into a girlish grin. "Things are getting back to normal. We're even having a new surge of romance. It's very nice." I smile knowingly as we say our goodbyes.

After Sue makes a hurried exit to work I sit down to ponder the good news. Waves of relief flow through me as I thank God that Philip has pulled out of his long bout with depression. I always believed he would, but it hurt to see him unhappy for so many years. Now I know that our prayers have been answered.

At the second week in August our entire family returns from their wanderings to celebrate Harry's mother's ninetieth birthday. Memere, as the family calls her, invites over fifty friends and all her relations to a catered party at the local women's club. She is the oldest of eleven children so the number of relatives is considerable.

Exuding more energy than reasonable for a five-foot great grandmother who walks with a cane, 'Mem' thrives on parties, the bigger the better. She makes her own arrangements with a caterer then asks, "Would you mind hanging up a few balloons around the hall so it won't look so bare?" The family goes all out for her with floral arrangements on tables, crepe paper streamers and banners about the walls, and helium balloons tied to the backs of chairs. Of course there's a special birthday cake, a giant decorated sheet cake with two candles in the center shaped '9' and '0'. Her face beams as she stands over her cake at the front of the hall while a hundred people sing 'Happy Birthday'.

Peter captures the gala event with his new camcorder. After the last speech is made and the hall empties out, we gather up the remains of the feast and return home to watch the party on video. I kick off my high heels and prop my feet up on the coffee table. When the film ends we remain sprawled about the living room resting. Philip gets up and walks out to the kitchen. Soon I hear cupboard doors bang and pots and pans rattle. "He can't be hungry already," I think. I'm even more puzzled when he comes back carrying my aluminum mixing bowl.

His face reveals a sly grin as though he possesses a secret no one else is privy to. Looking around the room he announces, "As long as we're all together, why don't we draw names for our Christmas gift exchange?" At first the kids look surprised. Christmas is over four months away. As the idea takes hold we begin to agree.

"That's a brilliant idea. We won't all be together again before Christmas." We find a couple of sheets of lined school paper and Philip prints out each person's name, spacing them a couple of inches apart so they can be cut out and put into the bowl for the "secret drawing". The others go through the names counting on their fingers to make sure everyone is represented.

"I already know what I'm going to put on my wish list," Philip says with an elfin twinkle in his eye. I get out more sheets of paper and some pencils so we can all write down what we want for Christmas. During the year, ideas for useful and appealing gifts I would like for Christmas pop into my head, but when this moment comes I cannot think of a single item. I look up to see others staring blankly, chewing on their pencils.

Philip folds the names into quarter inch squares and tosses them around in the bowl. We look stealthily at the name we draw, then tuck it away in pocket or purse so no one will find out till Christmas from whom they are getting a present.

"Okay," Peter says picking up his camcorder, "everybody outside for the 'line-up'." The "line-up" is a specific group pose of the nine children exactly like one I had taken to put on Christmas cards twenty-two years ago. There's a rush to get cameras so everyone can get a shot of this and we laugh and jostle our way out the front door. Philip dances a tango down the front steps while Peter films him. Feelings of warm, satisfying pleasure fill me when we are all together having fun. I have no reason to think these happy times will ever end.

35

⇜ 3 ⇝

Where's Philip

By mid-September our attic project nears completion. After working the night shift at the hospital all week I sorely need my weekend off. Desire for 'R & R' vies for attention with odd jobs on my list. Various tasks run through my head as I hurry along to the Employee's exit. "If I finish painting the attic this weekend, Mike can coat the floor boards with Polyurethane during the week. "

Engrossed in my planning I'm startled by an elderly Sister of Charity nun standing at the doorway holding a large bunch of long stemmed crimson carnations. With a nod of greeting she presses a flower into my hand. My surprised look prompts her to explain, "It's in honor of St. Vincent de Paul's feast day this Sunday, September 27th. He's the founding father of our order, you know." The wrinkles at the corners of her mouth deepen with obvious pleasure as she imparts this bit of information. I suspect the Sisters have special perks in store for themselves this weekend.

I thank her for the flower and push my way through the door. Crabby complaints start barreling through my thoughts. "I'll bet St. Vincent would treat his employees better than you do," I mutter quietly. Right now I'm disgruntled with hospital management for delaying my promotion to Clinical Nurse II. I've been doing the work for a year and a half. Now I feel I deserve the pay and title that go with it.

During my fifteen-minute drive home, I consider arguments I can use to secure that position when next I encounter my supervisor. Before falling into bed I prop the carnation in a glass of water on the windowsill over the kitchen sink. By now, the inoffensive flower has come to represent my conflict with the hospital.

Shortly after two in the afternoon I snap awake, still ruminating on my problems at work. "I'm going to call my supervisor right now and have it out with her," I decide.

"No!" comes a faint voice from somewhere inside me.

Stubbornly I argue with this warning voice, "But I have a right to discuss this with her."

"No!" the mysterious voice repeats insistently in my mind.

I choose to ignore this warning, pull on my slippers and robe and walk to the phone by the living room couch. My supervisor answers her page immediately. We fence verbally for half an hour. Out of the corner of my eye I see Harry making waving motions at me trying to get my attention. When at last I finish the conversation he says, "Well, it's about time you hung up. You're supposed to call Sue at this number." He hands me a scrap of paper.

With my brain still echoing from the words of the last phone call, I stare at the unfamiliar number. The only Sue that comes to mind is a nurse I work with on the night shift. As I dial I wonder idly if she wants to switch hours with me.

"Hello, DVR, Sue Olive speaking." Her voice startles me.

"Oh, it's you. I didn't recognize your phone number."

"I'm at work. The reason I'm calling is that I'm worried about Phil. I've been trying to call him at home all day and I don't get any answer." She speaks rapidly, emphasizing the last four words.

I struggle to gather mental faculties together to deal with this new piece of information. "Oh . . well, he could be outside working."

"He could be, but he would have come in for lunch. I tried all during my lunch hour. I couldn't get him." I notice a tremble in her voice as she continues. "I have this feeling that something is wrong. We had a confrontation last night... about his drinking again."

"Oh, no! I had no idea he started drinking again." Her words slam into the dam of hope I've built up during the summer months. "He looked so happy lately," I object. With illusions crumbling I feel my old worries about Philip pouring back in.

"Apparently he's been drinking all summer. I found boxes of empty beer cans in the basement, and this last month, I've seen him so drunk he could hardly walk. Last night I told him I couldn't live with him like this. We can work out our other problems, but alcohol feels like some evil force that comes between us. We said other angry things and finally he said, 'Don't worry, I won't be here when you get home tonight.'" Her voice breaks into a sob. "I have this terrible feeling . . . I'm afraid he's going to do something crazy . . . maybe even kill himself."

At that I rally. "Now, Sue, Phil would never do that," I assure her with the firmness of my convictions in my voice. "Maybe he decided to go back for inpatient treatment."

"I don't think so. I tried to take him to the inpatient clinic before I left for work this morning. He refused to go. I called his doctor a little while ago; he hasn't heard from Phil either. I thought maybe you could check with your kids. They might have seen him around the East Side house, or maybe at the university." The glimmer of hope steadies her voice.

"Don't worry, Sue. I'm sure he's all right. I'm going over to the house now to paint the attic. I'll find out if the kids have seen him. They've been at the university all day and might have run into him."

Before I say goodbye, I promise to call her as soon as I find out anything. During the fifteen-minute drive to the East Side I think fretfully about what can be done to help Philip. Where would he go if Sue refused to live with him? "Dear God, please help Philip. Keep him safe and heal him."

"I haven't seen Phil today, but I'm sure he's okay." Cathy smiles confidently when I relay Sue's concerns to her.

"Philip would never do anything like commit suicide," says Peggy. "He was here two days ago to pick up tools they've been using in the attic. He looked really happy. Said he was doing well in school and has decided to go right on to get his Master's."

"That's right," says Cathy. "He even joined the volleyball team at school and will be playing every Wednesday. He said he'd come over to visit us next week after the game."

Their reassurances confirm my own feelings that Philip is okay. "Have either of you seen Mike this afternoon?"

Cathy shakes her head. "No, I didn't run into him today and he hasn't gotten home from school yet. Maybe he's seen Phil today. Anyway, don't worry, Mom. I'm sure Phil is all right." Peggy agrees with her.

The girls head back into the kitchen where they're snacking and studying. "I'll be upstairs doing some painting in the attic," I call back as I climb the stairs.

For about an hour I roll gray sand-textured paint on the new attic wallboards, starting with the ceiling first. The ten-foot ceiling in Mike's living quarters is a challenge and a mess. The roller continually emits a fine gray drizzle as I balance on a ladder and paint over my head. I'm rolling as fast as I can ignoring the splatters so I can finish before supper time.

I hear the front doorbell ring. "Mom, there's someone here to see you," Cathy calls up to me.

I wipe off as much of the paint from my face and glasses as I can with the damp rag I keep handy, and climb down the ladder. From the second floor landing I see a tall, middle aged man with a receding hairline. He's standing in the front hallway. He is dressed in neat, but casual attire. A stranger. "One of our new neighbors," I think. Suddenly I feel embarrassed about my paint-spattered appearance. As I approach him I say, "Hello, you'll have to excuse my appearance. I've been painting."

He seems to take no notice of my disheveled attire. He looks at me solemnly for a few moments without speaking. Then . . . slowly . . . unmistakably . . . "Philip is dead," is all he says.

In the microseconds between each syllable sounding in my ears, my brain efficiently processes each word. PHILIP . . . my son . . whom I love; IS . . . not might be . . not, we think is; DEAD . . . not injured . . not critical . . not dying.

The stranger speaks again. "He took his own life." The words all come together in a jagged bolt. They pierce my consciousness and shatter forever the world as I've known it.

Cathy, standing in the hallway, screams.

"God! No!" I shout at this terrible apparition standing before me.

Peggy runs into the room, her eyes searching our faces for an explanation. "Philip is dead," Cathy and I cry out to her. Her face drains of color. Her mouth opens, but no sound comes out.

The tall man speaks. "I'm Father Ed from the retreat house. We found him in the garage. He was lying in the back of the pickup with the motor running. He must have been there a couple of hours."

Waves of shock and pain sear through me. "Oh, God! Oh, God, no!" is all I can say.

Father Ed continues, his face taut with determination, his arms held rigidly at his sides. "I drove out here to tell you because, well, we didn't want to tell you this over the phone."

"Thank you for coming," I manage to say between the sobs that wrench my body. "I know this wasn't easy for you."

He nods in agreement. "I'm very sorry," he says, then turns around to the door and leaves.

He leaves Cathy, Peggy, and me standing in the front hall staring at each other in confusion, not believing Philip is dead; yet knowing it is true. Cathy and I convulse with the intensity of our cries. Tears well up in Peggy's eyes but she is silent. We hang on to each other for support till we recover from the first wave of shock.

"We've got to tell the others," I say at last. Together we go to the second floor bedroom where Geri is resting for her night shift of private duty nursing. We wake her up. With great effort, I choose some words to deliver the terrible message. Telling Geri seems to force the horrible truth more deeply into my heart.

At first, waking from a sound sleep, she can't comprehend our words. Her expression is blank, her eyes dazed. I explain again, slowly, gently. Gently? How can you tell someone gently that their brother has committed suicide? As Geri's eyes fill with tears, the awareness hits me that this morbid news has to be told and retold to every member of the family . . to Harry, to the rest of the children . . . I have to phone the ones living out of town. There is no other way. And how are we going to tell Memere? She always loved Phil so dearly.

"He can't be dead, Mom." Geri's cries softly as we sit next to her on the bed and hold her. Then, comprehending the full meaning of our message she says, "He must have been in a lot of pain."

"I've got to go home and tell Dad." I notice that I'm still wearing my painting coveralls. I pull them off and roll them into a ball to carry under my arm. Forgotten, the open paint can in the attic and the unwashed roller in the pan harden into a gummy gray mass.

Cathy and Peggy decide to go to the university to look for Mike. Geri pulls on her clothes. "We'll come home when we all get back together." she decides for the rest of them.

Only long years of driving experience enable me to handle my car: shift the gears, turn the steering wheel just so, step on the brake at the right moment. I stare out through the windshield at the unreal world about me, at the familiar streets I have traveled so often. Shoppers, joggers, and workers hurry home for supper, move about as though nothing has happened. A group of teenage 'punks' all with brightly colored hair and garish clothing stare at me insolently, impatient for me to get out of their way at a crossing. "They don't know," I think. "How could they? Would they be kinder to me if they knew?"

Harry looks stunned as I tell him. "Is this some kind of sick joke?" I repeat my message. At first all he can do is shake his head in disbelief. Then his tears begin to flow. I hold on to him and we cry until our first flood of tears is exhausted. I repeat all that Father Ed told us about Philip's death.

"I'd better call Sue and see what we can do to help. Let's not call the rest of the family till we talk to her. We'll know more of the details then."

"On my way home I passed the ambulance taking Philip away," Sue tells me. "When I saw it my mouth went dry instantly. I knew right away he was dead." She draws in a couple of quick breaths. "The police called me at work and told me to come home right away. They wouldn't tell me what happened. The Sheriff was already in the house and was questioning Josh and Sarah without me. The kids didn't know what was going on. They were so scared."

"We're coming to your house as soon as Mike and the girls get here. Is there anything we can do? Can I bring some supper for you and the kids?"

"I couldn't eat anything and some friends of mine are here already. They're going to get stuff from McDonald's for the kids. There is something you can do though. Would you drive over and tell my mother? I don't want to tell her over the phone. I don't know how she's going to take this."

"Of course, I'll go right now. We'll see you in a little while." I explain to Harry what Sue asked me to do and go back out to the car. Sue's mother, Eleanor, was widowed a year ago and lives alone in her house at the southern edge of our suburb.

By the time I get to Eleanor's house she already has the news. Sue changed her mind and decided to call her. "I don't know how Sue can take this." Her brows and forehead wrinkle with worry. She squeezes her hands together spasmodically. "She's been through so much. Now she has to raise Josh and Sarah alone." We sit in her living room and cry together. She declines my offer of a ride to Sue's house. "I'd better stay here and call the rest of my family." Her words remind me of the painful task lying ahead of me.

By the time we get to Sue's, Chris and Karen are already there. Mike notified them as soon as he heard the news. Karen cries noisily as Chris holds her in his arms. Streams of tears flow down his cheeks. Sue's living room is crowded with crying people, all of them loyal friends of Philip.

A Franciscan Priest from their parish has come to offer spiritual support. He looks too young for the job, not even as old as Philip. But when he turns his fresh, smooth face my way I see a calm wisdom in his eyes.

Bags of McDonald's food are passed around. It's past suppertime but I can't eat anything. Neither can Harry or Sue. Josh downs a couple of hamburgers and a coke—a good sign. Sarah nibbles on french fries. They sit side by side on the couch, their eyes turned toward their Mom while they eat. The room is quiet while friends and family partake of the fast food supper. Sue begins telling us about the tragic events as they unfolded that afternoon. Her voice has taken on a nasal quality, her sinuses swollen from constant crying. I realize I must sound the same.

"The boy who helps Phil with the yard work found him in the garage just before Josh and Sarah got home from school. Sarah got home first and the boy made her call the ambulance. It was the ambulance driver, not the police, who called me at work and told me to come home. As soon as I got that call I knew my fears were real. I knew Phil was dead." She breaks down crying. We wait silently till she is able to continue.

"Phil had this all planned out. He didn't want me or the kids to be first to find him. He knew the boy was coming to help with the yard work this afternoon. That boy was the one that discovered Phil. They found his body stretched out in the back of the pick-up . . . just as if he had lain down to sleep. . . I don't know why he didn't answer the phone when I called him during my lunch hour. Frank said he talked to him around noon. He must have gone into the garage about one o'clock."

Sue stops to comfort Sarah who is making whimpering noises and wiping her eyes with a McDonald's napkin. Josh stops eating and starts to cry. Their distress stirs up her indignation. She says angrily, "I was so mad at the Sheriff. He started questioning the kids before I got home, before they had any idea what was happening. Then the ambulance drivers demanded to know where to take Phil's body. 'We have to know right away,' they said. 'You'll have to make a decision.' I couldn't think of what to say. They were all so rude."

Murmurs of disapproval rumble through the room. "That's terrible!" Cathy speaks up. "How mean of them."

"Yes, and the kids said the Sheriff came in and searched the house before I got here. I don't like the way they handled this at all."

My own temper flares hearing that Sue and the children were subjected to such crude treatment. I hear Chris's voice from a corner of the room. "What a bunch of jerks!"

Disgusted, Mike nods. "Not very professional. These country lawmen don't do much but give out speeding tickets and run off trespassers. When something like this comes up they don't know how to handle it." Mike's three years as a private detective gives him some expertise in these matters.

We do what we can to comfort Sue, which isn't very much; we are all devastated. We embrace, we cling together looking searchingly into each other's faces hoping to find some comfort, hoping to hear or to speak some perfect word or phrase that will make things all right again.

The Parish Priest does his best to console us with words of the Spirit. He tells us what a good person Phil was, and he is sure that he has at last found peace. When I have a chance to speak to him alone I express a fear that has been nagging me since my first shock of hearing about Philip's suicide. "I've been taught since grade school days about what a terrible sin it is to commit suicide. Is God going to punish Phil for taking his own life?"

"We've learned a lot since those days." He speaks gently but firmly with the assurance of a strong faith. "God isn't going to punish Philip for taking his own life. Philip was sick . . . very sick. He didn't get that way deliberately. He wanted so much to be well and strong. He was seeking a radical transformation." His words cut through the armor of my rigid moral training, but a lifetime of moral training does not die easily. A small, persistent doubt twists about in my conscience.

Before we leave Sue asks me, "What do you think Phil should be buried in? He has one good suit that he bought to wear to my father's funeral, but he never wore it after that. He always wore jeans and a flannel shirt or tee's. Maybe we should bury him in those."

Visions of past funerals run through my mind. The men are all lying in state dressed up in suits and ties. "I think it should probably be in a suit."

"You do? . . .Okay." I hear the note of disappointment in her voice.

I'm exhausted by the time we get home, but I know I must call the rest of the family. I can't stall any longer. I decide to start with our oldest child and work my way down. What can I say that will soften the blow . . somehow make the information I must pass on less shocking? I start with Judie and Jardo in Prairie Creek. Jardo answers the phone. "I have some very bad news," I begin. "Something terrible has happened." Without waiting for an answer I continue. "Philip is dead." I wait for the pause . . the crying out . . the protest of disbelief. "He took his own life this afternoon."

"I can't believe this. I just talked to him this week. We discussed plans for deer hunting. We talked about a design for a new hunting T-shirt."

I feel my chest tighten.I begin crying again. I speak haltingly, going on to explain the how and where of it. But not the 'why'. I don't understand 'why'. Jardo puts Judie on the phone. I repeat my message. The same shocked silence, the same denial, then crying, while I plod on with the details.

Next I call Peter and Jill. Jill answers first and I start my sad tale again . . then Peter . . then Mary and Mike. Each message I deliver sends me into another crying spell. All of the children say they will make arrangements to come home as quickly as possible.

I don't know how my Aunt Leone, already sickly and in her eighties will react to the news. I call her brother Ray, a priest, part of whose vocation it is to deal with the mournful aspects of life and death. They are both residents in the same home for the elderly. He takes the news well, as I knew he would. He promises to deliver the message in person to Leone in the morning.

The only person left to tell is Memere. Harry volunteers for this one. "I'll go to her house in the morning and break the news."

The last call I make is to a close friend from my church community. Bill has been a group counselor for twenty years and is a source of strength and advice for many of us. When I tell him what has happened to Philip he has the same reaction as my children. . . disbelief, then shock. Bill has come to know all of my family during the fifteen years I've known him. He knows first-hand what an important role each one plays in my life, especially Philip whose struggles with depression and drinking have been my continual concern for the last few years.

Immediately he's aware of the emotional devastation I'll be facing, more so than I myself can comprehend at this time. "You're going to need a lot of help to get through this." His voice sounds grave. "I want you to call me whenever you need to talk. Don't forget that. It doesn't matter what time it is. Call me anytime of the day or night." I promise I will call him when I need to talk. I couldn't foresee then how many times my struggle with grief would prompt me to dial his number.

I am drained of physical and emotional strength when I crawl into bed, but my brain will not quit reviewing the horrors of the day. With closed eyes I see the dripping grey roller moving across the ceiling, look down from the top of the stairs at the tall stranger in the hallway. I see the sun shining through the screen door behind him and his sorrowful expression as his lips move to tell me the news. I see alarm on the faces of my children, of Harry. I see their pain. I feel my pain anew. *Philip is dead.*

Grief is those three words, rising like a lump of leaven gone berserk, filling my thoughts, my emotions, spilling over into my body. My body strains under the weight of it. I'm hungry, but I can't eat with this lump in my throat, this knot in my stomach. Crying clogs up my sinuses and I gasp for air through my mouth making it parched, making me thirsty. I go to the bathroom for a glass of water to wet my mouth, I keep it handy on my dresser. I bunch up my pillows to prop up my head so I can breathe a little easier. I fall asleep.

My bedroom shade picks up a pale white color from the dawn sky. A sharp pain in my chest awakens me and reminds me that Philip is dead. I remember Sue's last words to me before we parted yesterday evening. "I feel like my heart is breaking."

4

❧ Vultures ❧

The late September sun, low in the East, slants into my Escort windows as I drive north on Highway 45 to pick up Sue at her home. Philip has been dead a little less than eighteen hours, but Sue is told she must arrange for his funeral and burial this morning. "Can you help me?" she asked in an SOS over the phone early this morning. "It's hard for me to think straight." My own senses are fogged with pain and lack of sleep, but I agree to accompany her to the funeral parlor.

There are few cars on the road this early on a Saturday. Driving seems effortless, automatic, allowing my mind to ponder the devastation into which our lives have plunged. Harry and I would have gone to the lakefront this morning to watch Mike compete in 'Al's Run'. It would have been his tenth year in the run. He's been training but he won't be running today, nor will we be watching.

I force my thoughts to today's task—a funeral. Sue has picked out a funeral parlor a few miles from their house. I try to picture Philip lying in a casket with his eyes closed, hands folded. A forceful realization strikes me. We can't bury him in a suit. He hated wearing suits. It wouldn't even look like him.

As soon as Sue gets into the car I tell her what I've decided about the suit. "I thought the same thing this morning. I didn't know how I was going to convince you." Philip's death generates a mysterious union between us. We find ourselves agreeing as we go through the options presented by the funeral director. We both seem to know exactly what kinds of goods and services Philip would like for his funeral.

We page through the folder containing memorial holy cards and both choose one with a strong profile of Christ on the front. For the back, I find a poem about wanting to go home to God to rest. It speaks poignantly to Philip's needs at the time of his death. Sue says it is perfect.

The director leads us into a large display room filled with caskets. Behind his back we eye each other with raised brows as he points out the fifty-five hundred dollar bronze model guaranteed leak proof for a full century. So who's going to check? We both know Phil would prefer a wooden casket. He loved making things out of wood ever since he was a small boy. We pick out a simple hardwood casket polished to gleaming honey brown. It feels like we're buying lovely presents for Phil. If only he weren't dead.

We follow the director back to his office. There

are papers to sign, the death certificate, the wording for the obituary. He is cordial and gentle throughout the arrangements and seems apologetic when he requires Sue to sign an agreement to pay for everything.

"His wallet, watch, and other valuables we found in his pocket are in this envelope," he says handing a small brown envelope to Sue. Then he picks up a large grocery bag from the floor next to his desk. "These are the clothes he was wearing when he died." He holds the bag out to Sue. She shudders and shakes her head.

"I don't want them." She looks repulsed by the idea.

"I'll take them." I hold out my arms to receive these remnants of my dead son, cradling them in my lap.

Our next chore is picking out the grave site. Sue directs me to Saint Francis country cemetery where she has arranged to meet the caretaker. A stocky, ruddy complexioned man in a blue work shirt and stained, baggy overalls greets us when we arrive. His thinning, sun bleached hair blows askew in the wind. He is polite, but his earthy, matter of fact speech sharply contrasts with the polished manner of the impeccably dressed funeral director we've just left. "We got lots of empty spaces here," he says with a sweeping wave of his arm. Just look around and pick out a spot and I'll measure it off for ya."

The sun, high in the South, warms my neck and shoulders as we trek across the grass, weaving about the gravestones. The tension in my back and shoulders is easing. Sue looks at me, her brown eyes squinty in the sunshine. "Phil always said he wanted to be buried under a tree. He didn't even want to be in a casket. He worried about the environment, you know. 'I want to return to the soil quickly,' he used to say." I shake my head. Philip was always so impossibly idealistic.

"There's a big tree over in the middle." I point to an oak tree in a section of the cemetery not yet being used.

"But, there's no one buried over there. We like being with people." We walk among the grave sites for another ten minutes until Sue says, "How about this small pine tree near the road. It will grow to be very big in a few years and there's room for a grave for each of us."

"This looks like a very good spot. Lots of people buried around here too." Sue shows the spaces she wants to the caretaker who has been following us around patiently. He jots some notes on his clipboard, then pulls a tape measure out of his back pocket. When he looks up from his figures his eyes are caught by something in the distance behind our backs.

" 'Scuse me a minute." A frown clouds his pleasant, rugged features. He looks across a small road that bisects the cemetery, to a section where two workmen are preparing to dig a new grave. One of them motions with his arms and calls him. He walks over, looks at the spot where they're pointing, takes his tape measure and makes some quick calculations. He talks rapidly to the two diggers as he marks out a slightly different position for the grave.

"That was a close call," he says when he rejoins us. "We nearly buried Louise right on top of her husband Harold."

Sue and I can't help laughing. The dark sadness in her eyes momentarily sparks with merriment. "That's the kind of joke Phil would have liked," she says.

During the fifteen minute drive back to her house I begin to feel uneasy about leaving her alone with Josh and Sarah. "Are you going to be okay? I mean alone in the house with the kids?"

"I won't be alone. Our friends are taking turns staying with me. There's someone at the house now with Josh and Sarah." I nod in approval. I've charted pages of 'Nurses Notes' in my patients' charts about their psycho-social environment. Those with strong support groups and satisfying relationships tend to recover more quickly. Sue and the kids will make it through this. They have a loyal group of neighbors and friends to help them. Some of them go back as far as their high school years.

I pull my visor down to shield my eyes from the sun as I turn my Escort south on the expressway and head for home. Without Sue's presence and the concentration required by the morning's activities, pain oozes back into me from all sides, and thoughts of Philip's death overtake me.

I attempt to stabilize my emotions, forming a prayer in my mind. "Dear God . . . ." I begin again, "Oh. Jesus . . ." My spirit recoils in pain and confusion. "You let Philip die!" is all that comes to my mind. Even as a child I felt God close by, as though ready at my fingertips—a tangible force in my life. Not always granting my requests, but always present to listen and understand. Today a wall rises between us—a barrier high and steep. A barrier I do not wish to breach. Certain God was going to heal Philip, I feel betrayed . . tricked into a complacent hopefulness. I no longer trust Him.

Mike, Geri, Cathy and Peggy are all home when I return. We are all crying. . .all except Peggy. Her eyes are sad and she looks pale. She says she hasn't slept or eaten. She complains of feeling cold. I offer her the quilt from the bed in the spare room and she curls up with it in the rocking chair.

Peggy is registering the classic symptoms of shock. I'm well acquainted with this psychological defense mechanism that comes to our aid during times of tragedy. It spares us emotional trauma we're not strong enough to deal with; nature's shot of Novocain to the brain. I observed it in full bloom in disaster victims who strolled calmly away from death and destruction after a tornado. It's impossible to say how long it's safe to stay enveloped in this emotional vacuum. If Peggy gets stuck in it to the detriment of her health, we'll have to get professional help to unlock buried emotions.

Chris and Karen come in the afternoon. The others straggle in from their long journeys throughout the afternoon and evening. It's always the same. We say 'hello', kiss and embrace, and then we cry. Some, especially the children, are hungry. I don't have to worry about cooking. Gifts of casseroles, Jell-O's, rolls, and desserts begin arriving, along with sympathetic greetings from friends and neighbors. I begin nibbling at Jell-O's and pasta salads which slip down easily. They're the first food I've gotten down since Philip's death.

Now and then someone verbalizes the grievous thoughts that keep circling around in our heads like vultures. Cathy stands frowning at the center of the living room, hands on hips, head shaking, long brown hair whisking about, "I still can't believe Philip would kill himself. He was at our house Wednesday afternoon smiling and joking, talking about going for his Master's in Chemistry."

Geri looks up at her thoughtfully. "When I took Psych in nursing school they warned us about depressed patients who suddenly become unusually happy. That's when they might be planning suicide."

"I remember learning that, too." I nod. "They become happy because they believe they've found a way to end their misery."

Cathy continues shaking her head. "I can't believe Philip was thinking about that when he was visiting us last week."

"I've been thinking of a dream I had about Philip Wednesday night." The children stare at me. "He walked in our front door and I went over to greet him. He put his arms around me in a long embrace. In my dream I was surprised because he hasn't been very demonstrative the last few years. I could feel waves of love flowing between us. It was so real I woke up feeling happy. I believed then that he was cured; that he'd gotten over his depression. Now, I think . . I think he came to say goodbye."

Peter, with his scientific orientation, has a hard time swallowing that one. "I don't know, Ma." He frowns at me. "This whole thing is so unreal. Phil stuck with things no matter what. It wasn't like him to hang it up like this."

Mary looks at him, a questioning look in her soft hazel eyes, "I know what you mean. I always looked up to him… the strong one of the family. When he made up his mind to do something he wouldn't quit till he was finished."

"Yeh, that's how he was," Peter agrees. "I'll never forget that 'Hunger Hike' he went on right after he started high school. Jeez! Never thought he'd walk the whole thirty miles."

"I didn't either", Harry says. "I made sure he had a quarter so he could call us when he was ready to be picked up. He had blisters on his feet by the time he got home."

"I made him soak in a hot tub, but he was stiff and sore for days," I add.

"That's what I mean." Cathy continues to look defiant. "He was so dedicated to whatever he was working on that not even pain stopped him."

Mary sighs deeply. "He was always doing stuff like that. I thought he was going to do something spectacular with his life. Maybe even, somehow, make the world a better place for the rest of us."

I begin choking with sobs. "I know. I did too."

Philip's obituary makes it into the Sunday morning paper, a tribute to the efficiency of the funeral director and the typesetters. A newspaper friend of ours complained that obituaries are the bane of the typesetting profession. Received haphazardly until the moment of printing, they must continually shift articles around on several pages to accommodate them.

Harry and I aren't prepared for the shock the tiny bold letters of Philip's name send through us. Olive, Philip J., of Erin, age 33 yrs. . . I can't read any further for a while. We sit on our chairs by the kitchen table and weep, the newspaper spread open before us. The sunshine pours through our East window in gay yellow streams, illuminating the slim three-inch column of words we are staring at. The sun has been all wrong. It has been shining crazily bright ever since Philip died when there ought to have been glowering black clouds overhead.

By now we all believe Philip is dead, but it's knowledge we've carried about only in our minds and hearts, and shared with each other in the unseen world of verbal interchange. The printed words add a new dimension. They connect it to our visual world, making it astonishingly real. When I'm able, I finish reading the article. Yes, it's all correct.

We leave the paper open on the kitchen table for all to see. As the children shuffle over to read it I see them crumple in sorrow. Harry wonders if it would be better to fold up the paper and hide it. At first it sounds like the kindest thing to do, but some remote instinct grabs me and tells me it will be better to let truth unfold where it will.

The wake starts at six o'clock this evening. I stand in front of my closet wondering what would look appropriate and still be comfortable. I feel we are being hurtled into this funeral sequence at breakneck speed; I can't even decide what to wear. Harry puts on his new dark gray trousers and manages to squeeze into his old gray striped jacket one more time. There's some discussion among the girls. What would be suitable attire for a wake? I overhear Peggy, "It's like getting dressed for a party only you have to be careful not to look too festive."

Walking into the funeral parlor I'm struck with a feeling of reverence and the need to whisper. I wonder vaguely if it comes in deference to the quiet needed by those grieving, or if I sense the spirits of the dead still hovering about. My primary need is to see Philip. I push my way past small groups of mourners, my eyes fixed on the gleaming coffin at the far end of the room. I see the floral arrangements atop and surrounding it are September colors, including large branches of leaves turning into their reds and golds for Fall. I'm sure Sue planned them. Philip would be pleased.

Holding my breath I look down fearfully at this first sight of my dead child. Yes. The still form in the wooden casket looks exactly like Philip. He is wearing one of his newer red plaid flannel shirts and his best pair of jeans. Now there can be no doubt, no hiding of the truth. It is Philip, and he is dead.

Even in death he looks handsome, healthier than

he looked during the last years of his life. His blond hair is combed just so, without wisps that often freed themselves at his cowlick to face in the wrong direction. His beard is neatly trimmed. His fingers, twined with his brown Rosary, still have nicks and scrapes on them. His nails are short and split from the rough work he did. About his neck is the Cursillo cross that he loved, representing the spiritual group that gave him support during his last difficult years. We all loved him so much. "Oh, God. Why did you let him die?" my heart cries. No answer penetrates the blackness.

After a long while I tear my gaze away from him. One of Philip and Sue's closest friends stands next to me. "I've known him since I was fifteen years old." She looks down into the coffin with fondness in her eyes. "We had such lofty ideals in those days. We were going to change the world. Philip never let go of those dreams, but he couldn't make them come true. I think that's what killed him. He was one of the finest people I ever knew."

Her words renew the flood of tears to my eyes. "He wanted the world to be perfect. He wanted people to be perfect too, himself included. Things just aren't that way." She nods slowly, her eyes now staring into the long ago.

I'm surprised to see Sue's sister standing near the casket sobbing. She lives in Ohio and didn't see Philip very often. She returns my gaze and approaches. "He was so kind, so sensitive, but he held too much inside. I tried to draw him out. I told him he had to talk things out, get his feelings out in the open, but he never could."

"None of us knew how much he was hurting inside. Not Harry. not I, not any of his brothers or sisters, except. . . I think his sister Geri knew. If the rest of us had known we might have been able to help him." A thought creeps in as we stand together weeping. I tell myself, "If only I had been more sensitive to his feelings, I would have known how desperate he was. I could have found some way to save him." Remorse begins seeping into my soul like swamp water.

Philip's friend, Frank, comes over and looks at us with dark, sad eyes. "Things are never going to be the same again for me. Phil was my best friend."

"I'm sorry, Frank," was all I could think of to say.

I see Jardo standing alone off to one side. He's another one who doesn't readily share his feelings with others. Judie and Jardo were eighteen years old when they started dating, Philip was fourteen. Except for Judie, Philip was the member of our family that struck the closest friendship with Jardo. I stand next to a huge bouquet, partially hidden while I gaze at Jardo across the room. I let my thoughts drift back nineteen years to the day I first met this young man who was to play a significant role in Philip's life.

At first I didn't realize that 'Yardo' was spelled 'Jardo', short for Jaroslav. He was born in Czechoslovakia during the Communist turmoil that followed World War II in that part of Europe. His father, wishing to escape to a place of freedom, brought his wife and six-year old Jardo to the United States.

As he spent more time at our house he became popular with the children, especially Philip whose mind was ever searching for new ideas. Jardo was a history major at the university, an idealist, and a social reformer. Philip listened eagerly and the two of them joined in lengthy conversations. Cementing their friendship were the anti-war sentiments of that violent summer of '68; sentiments that fueled an anti-establishment fire in them which was never completely extinguished.

"Mom?" I look up to see Judie peering at me through the floral arrangement. I think she has been talking to me.

"Jardo looks like he's hurting a lot."

"He's taking this awfully hard. He was very close to Philip. Even closer than I was." I stare at her in surprise. "It's true. They sensed each other's deepest feelings, and could talk about them. Jardo couldn't do that with many people." We both gaze at him with mournful eyes, our empathy bridging the expanse of the room to reach out to him. "This is too hard, Mom. Philip shouldn't have done this." I shake my head, beginning to comprehend the far reaching effects of Philip's suicide.

Friends from my church community have traveled out to this country place to comfort me. They sent a bouquet of roses which graces the front corner of the room on a tall golden stand near the casket. They've only met Philip a few times. Most of them aren't sure what to say, but I'm touched by their caring. My friend, now counselor, Bill, is among them. He always knows what to say. His brow creases with worry lines as he inquires about my health. He talks with Peter who is standing nearby about the stress I'm under and how I will need lots of tender loving care. Bill worries about me while I worry about everybody else.

I make my way around the room talking with clusters of friends and neighbors who have come to mourn with us. I feel an aching in my chest, but I'm not aware of weariness or hunger. Only continual thirst breaks into my consciousness. I make my way frequently to the small lounge where water and coffee are available. My nursing orientation makes me wonder about the volume of body fluid lost by crying.

I'm surprised to see one of the nurses I work with on the night shift approaching me. During our breaks we've shared stories and pictures of our families and over the years have come to feel acquainted with all of them. She looks shocked as she stares at Philip. "I . . I couldn't believe it was your son. I saw the obituary this morning. But all the other names fit, so I figured it had to be you." She doesn't yet know that he took his own life because, of course, the obituary doesn't go into those details. I haven't talked to my co-workers about Philip's alcoholism and depression so now I must explain the whole tragic story. It's not easy. I think about how hard it will be going back to work—having to talk to others about Philip's death.

Our friend, Father Tom, comes over to stand next to me as I return for a final look at Philip. He's been deeply involved in Philip's struggles for the last few years. Seeing the distress of my final goodbye's to Phil, my last longing look at him, he says, "You'll always have the good memories of him."

"I don't want memories," I cry. "I want all of him."

We have arranged to hold the funeral mass at Holy Hill, the church Philip helped clean and maintain during the early years of his marriage. Sue insisted it take place in the larger, more ornate 'Upper Church'. "We can't do that," the funeral director told her. "We always hold funerals in the 'Lower Church' because the casket won't fit into the elevator."

"Then we'll carry it up the stairs." Sue can be very assertive. So the pallbearers, brothers Peter, Mike, and Chris, and brothers-in-law Jardo and Mike, with Philip's friend, Frank carry the casket up the steep outer stairway atop the great hill, and across the open walkway to the 'Upper Church'.

Uncle Ray, Father Tom, and the Pastor of Saint Mary's of the Hill parish will concelebrate the funeral mass and are already robed and up around the altar as we arrive. The Carmelite Fathers and Brothers of Holy Hill, and the priests Philip had gotten to know at the retreat house are in attendance. From my pew in the second row I turn to watch the church filling with friends and neighbors. There are so many clergymen it looks like solemn High Mass on a Holy Day. The sun, shining through the stained glass windows, lights up the sanctuary casting brightly colored shadows across the entire church, giving it a quality of heavenly splendor.

A group of Philip's old friends from his Tai Chi days on Brady Street, stands in front of me, to the right of the altar. They were in high school when they met, only fifteen years old. Full of idealism and promise, they dedicated themselves to ending the war in Vietnam and eliminating violence, racism, and environmental destruction from the face of the earth. They would be the generation that would, at last, heal the world's wounds. Today they play guitars and lead the singing. The anguish of their loss, their broken dreams, is in their music and I have never heard them sing more beautifully.

Father Gerard, the pastor, opens his homily with the words, "In THE ROAD LESS TRAVELED Dr. M. Scott Peck tells of a man who complained to him about how difficult his life was. Dr. Peck replied to him, 'Life is always difficult. It's difficult for everyone.' 'Oh, is that so?' the man questioned thoughtfully. 'Well, if life is difficult for everyone, I guess that makes me feel better . .'"

Father Gerard continues, "What most people don't realize is that for one quarter of the world's population, life is extremely difficult. Life was extremely difficult for Philip."

"How well he knew my boy."

Sue told me that Father Gerard was new to the parish but he and Philip had hit it off right from the start. Having been in Vietnam, Father had seen first hand the destructiveness of war and, like Philip, had become a protester against injustice and violence.

Father goes on to tell of Philip's sensitivity in caring for the poor and hungry of the Parish. "He organized the Human Concerns committee to collect money, used clothing, and food for them. He begged for and borrowed the typewriters and office supplies to prepare newsletters which reached out to more people. He struggled to pass on his own concern for the hungry people throughout the world. The pain of the world's suffering crushed in on him to a point he could no longer stand, and in that agony of pain he ended his life."

During the Offertory that follows I watch Sue, who is sitting in front of me suddenly stop crying. She stares up at the large Crucifix above the altar in a trance. After the service she tells me, "When I looked up at the Crucifix I saw Philip on it. While I watched, he was released from his suffering and taken up to Heaven."

There is consolation in her words and in those of Father Gerard. There's healing in the beauty of the ceremony and the great crowd that has come to offer their prayers for Philip and for us. As we walk together down the aisle toward the back exit I feel a surge of hope for our future happiness and am able to join in singing the words to the hymn HE WILL RAISE YOU UP ON EAGLES WINGS. I don't feel pain, but outside Bill tells me I'm walking hunched over as though I've just received a blow to the stomach.

The funeral procession doesn't take long, just a mile and a half down the country road to the Cemetery. We gather around the prepared site next to the small pine tree and the pallbearers rest the casket on the platform built over the grave. In the distance I see the twin steeples of Holy Hill church, the same ones Philip was climbing on and painting just a few short years ago. I lean over and speak to Harry quietly. "This is a perfect place for Philip to be buried."

His red rimmed eyes look off toward the distant spires. "I suppose so." His shoulders bend forward with the weight of it. His chest caves.

Birds are flitting about singing, insects are humming, two chestnut horses romp in a field across the road. Even the sky is a glorious blue. Clearly, nature is not grieving today, and for a few moments my spirit lifts on the warm Fall breeze.

When we're circled around the grave. Uncle Ray says a few prayers and we take turns blessing Philip's enclosed body with holy water. First Sue, Josh, and Sarah . . . then Harry and I, then Phil's eight brothers and sisters . . . then Sue's mother and sisters followed by the pall bearers and a few close friends. Philip is well blessed. The bright sun turns the holy droplets into showers of diamonds falling onto his polished wooden box.

Then it's time to go. We all walk away, and we leave Philip there.

The slow procession of cars takes us back to the Parish Center at the foot of Holy Hill church where parish members have prepared a buffet dinner. I'm amazed that such a feast has been served up on such short notice. While the guests fill their plates Sue sits dejectedly at the end of one of the long tables talking to a friend. I overhear the friend telling her sternly, "Of course, he loved you. You shouldn't have any doubts about that."

"But I can't remember him saying so, not for years."

I butt into the conversation. "Sue, it wasn't six months ago that Phil told me he loved you ten thousand times more than the day he married you."

"He said that?"

"Those were his exact words."

Her face brightens. "He never said anything like that to me. I wonder why?" We all wonder why. Why don't we tell people that we love them? I can't remember the last time I told Philip that I loved him . . . or Harry . . . not our other children. I resolve to tell them this very day. But not Philip. It's too late to tell Phil.

Once more I feel remorse twisting about. How many times had I looked lovingly at Philip but never spoken the words? If only I had said them it might have kept him going. How I wish now I had said, "I love you."

I notice that Sue isn't eating. I fix plates for both of us with small scoops of Jell-O, fresh fruit, and pastas made slippery with mayonnaise. I sit down next to her coaxing her to eat. "This looks good." She starts nibbling at the food. "I'm glad you didn't bring me anything heavy."

While the guests finish eating I walk between the

long tables stopping to talk to those I haven't yet greeted. Among them is a girl Philip dated in high school. I don't recognize her at first with her long blond hair bobbed short. She introduces herself telling me they were in the same chemistry class at the university last semester. "What a brain he had. He got A's in all his exams while the rest of us struggled to get B's and C's. His death is such a waste. He had so much potential."

I get choked up again. "Yes, a terrible waste." Some of Philip's friends are not that direct. They talk about the fine funeral service, the unusually warm weather, the delicious food, but avoid the central issue. Philip is dead. I understand. They are still shocked, wanting to hide the truth from themselves, from me. There is time. It will come to them.

I recognize one of Philip's long time friends with his wife sitting next to him. They're picking at their food between tears. This young couple is still recovering from a tragedy of their own. Two years earlier their three-year-old daughter drowned at their lake cottage.

"It's good of you to come" I say. "This must be hard on you after . . . well, after what happened . . ."

". . You mean after Kelly drowned?" Jim fills in. "It's okay to talk about it. We like to talk about Kelly. Somehow it keeps her with us a little longer."

"We love renewing her memory," Kathy adds, "and strangely, we don't mind talking about how she died. I know it sounds crazy, because it invariably makes us cry."

"I'm beginning to find that out in these few hours since Philip died. Even though his death is so painful I want to keep talking about him. But. . well, I sense that some others are afraid to say his name, or admit that we're here at his funeral."

"You're going to find that a lot," Jim nods knowingly. "Most people don't know what to say. They're afraid of hurting you even more."

"Since Kelly's death we've both realized that there's nothing anyone can say that could possibly make us feel worse. And. . . the fact that they're willing to share our pain and listen to our Kelly stories makes us feel a whole lot better."

"Sometimes we cry when someone talks about Kelly, but I tell them that's okay. Tears wash out the pain that gets stuck inside."

"I'm very glad you told me this. Now I know what I can say to these dear people who seem embarrassed." We embrace with long, warm hugs, and share more tears before I move on.

Father Tom comes to visit us the following morning, as if sent by God to answer the agonizing question that permeates our thoughts and rises frequently to our lips. "One thing you're going to keep doing is asking 'Why?'. We don't know why. I do know that Philip was very sick."

"But he was such a spiritual person," my voice rises with pleading. "He prayed all the time for healing. We've all been praying for him for years. Why didn't God give him some peace and happiness?"

"I don't know why," he answers me gently. "It doesn't do any good to ask why. You can stack up the whys from now to eternity and you'll never understand it until you get there."

It's sound advice but, of course, we don't follow it. 'Whys' like vultures continue to circle about our heads, frequently descending to tear us to pieces. As the days, weeks, and months, go by, I torment myself for long periods of time searching for what went wrong.

❧ 5 ☙

The Attic

"Phil had great ideas when it came to solving the problems we ran into." Mike and I are up in the newly remodeled attic nailing cherry-stained strips of finishing woodwork around the patio doors and windows. He has me hold them in place while he drives the nails. "I was planning on getting his help with this finishing work. I'm not sure how to fit the molding pieces into these oddly shaped corners." I hear an unspoken resentment in his tone of voice. Philip has abandoned him.

I catch his sideways glance. "Philip's death ruined a lot of people's plans. Yours are probably the least of them." My terse reply startles both of us. I sound harsh lately. I'm not sure why. After a few seconds Mike nods, then turns his face away from me. I'm thinking about Sue and the children. Perhaps he is too.

Mike leaves to attend his class at the university. Alone in the attic, I'm putting the final coat of polyurethane on the thick pine floorboards we've sanded and cleaned—my last task in the attic remodeling project. How good it would be to show Philip the fine quality of the finished rooms. Without Phil, Mike would have had a rough time building the elevated platform/bedroom floor, or resetting roof beams so the ceiling would be straight.

The last time I saw Philip alive was in this attic room. He was on a ladder, his stained jeans hanging low on his slim hips, leaning precariously over the stairwell while fastening a piece of drywall to the ceiling. He showed no fear of the twenty-foot drop between himself and the stairs. Agile and relaxed, ladder-tops seemed to be his natural habitat.

Just before I left that day I said, "Phil, I sure appreciate your help here. We couldn't have done it without you. Can I pay you something for the work you've done, maybe give you some equity in the house?"

"You can give me some interest-free money when I buy my land."

"It's a deal," I said going down the stairs waving a goodbye to him perched high above me.

I see his ladder standing in the corner. He forgot to take it home the day he picked up his tools. Or maybe he already knew he would never need it again. "I wonder if Sue can use it? I should take it back to her," I think walking toward it. As I put my hands on one of the lower rungs, the pain of loss hits me at once. The presence of my son clings to that ladder.

My cry echoes through the empty room. "Okay,

Philip, you can come back now. We need you back here. We need you now!" I cry for a long time caressing the splintery wooden rung. "There is no way back for you, is there? This is the end of your being with us. This is no good, Phil, being cut off from you like this. Death is no good."

I pour out every bit of my remaining energy varnishing those last few floorboards. When I get back home I find Harry slumping in his lounge chair looking teary-eyed. His expression shows me he's been having a difficult grieving day too. "I've been thinking about all this garbage," he starts out, then stops abruptly and shakes his head. "Oh, never mind. What's the use in talking about it? Philip's gone and nothing will bring him back."

"Sometimes it helps to talk. Tell me what you've been thinking about."

"Forget it." Neither of us forgets it, but nothing I say encourages him to share his feelings. Harry's morose silence is all that speaks to me of his thoughts. 'Philip is dead' underlies our every move.

I'm invited to a late movie by Bill and some of our church friends. I can't keep my mind on the film, but it feels good to be with friends and talk with them. The sadness goes away for a while.

That night I dream that Philip is dead and we need pallbearers. We need them in sets of three. More and more people keep volunteering until a large room is crowded with them. Then I look out the window to the top of a grassy hill in the distance. The sun is shining and the sky is a dazzling blue.

Three people come walking over the top of the bright green hill, then another three. I know they are coming to help. "Now Philip has enough help," says Bill who is suddenly standing by my side in the dream. I feel a sense of peace, as though all our troubles have been taken care of. I wake up feeling happy.

When I tell Bill about my dream he's not surprised. "You may have more of those kinds of dreams. We call them healing dreams. Many people who have suffered a great loss experience them. They'll help you." I look forward to having more dreams.

Judie calls in the afternoon. She's come from Prairie Creek with her three daughters and is staying with Sue. "I'm helping Sue harvest Phil's garden. I wondered if you'd like to come out and help us?" After consulting with Harry we volunteer to drive out to help.

Philip has a lush garden. It's a small plot, about forty by sixty feet at the edge of the acre of lawn that surrounds the retreat house. The soil is richly fertilized and heavily planted. Phil always said cow manure makes the best fertilizer. This, after earning forty-two credits in chemistry and agriculture. He has also faithfully mulched his plot year after year with the falling leaves.

Italian tomatoes in abundance have ripened faster than they could be harvested and lay red and rotting on the ground. We carefully pick the few that have not spoiled and lay them out in a shallow box. We pick what remains of the lettuce, green peppers, cucumbers, squash, pumpkins, and celery. Judie's daughters, Theresa and Jessica, help Sarah pile the vegetables in boxes and haul them to the root cellar in an old red wagon. Our granddaughter Michelle works alongside Harry and me.

We dig delicately with spades and hand trowels to unearth the carrots without damaging them, then the radishes, which are firm and as big as golf balls. Sue points out the garlic growing at the edge of the plot and we dig that up too. I pick and pull and dig in awe and reverence for the work of our son's hands.

I hear a groaning sound coming from Harry's direction and I see him standing erect and stretching out his back muscles. He shuffles over to a tree stump and sits down to smoke a cigarette. Judie has been digging up the red potatoes and Idaho's over in the potato patch. As I walk over to help her I glance down regretfully at my new white Addida's, now streaked with dirt and manure. Clumps of the rich soil cling to the edges of my soles as I walk. I frown, thinking I should have worn my old brown Hush Puppies for this kind of work. An involuntary sigh escapes me. What's the difference? Spoiling a new pair of shoes? Philip's death has already ruined our lives.

For a few minutes I watch Judie who has filled four grocery boxes with potatoes. I ask her, "Why did Philip kill himself when he was such a good gardener?"

She jams the spade point down into the dirt and stands up next to it. "I don't know. I don't understand how he could leave all these good things he had. His own wife and children, this beautiful home, his friends and family." She raises her brows bewildered. "What could have made him so sad he had to kill himself and leave all this?"

"I don't know what. It doesn't make sense. I've been thinking about it so much these last few days I'm getting very absent minded. Can't seem to remember anything from one minute to the next."

"I'm doing the same thing. I keep driving past streets I'm supposed to turn down and past places I meant to stop. I have to turn around and go back."

Sue hears us talking. "I guess I'm not the only absent minded one these days. I was speeding down County Line Road when I got stopped by a cop. I completely forgot to watch the speedometer. When I told him my husband committed suicide last week he let me off with a warning. I've got to be more careful."

We help her load a heavy grocery box full of potatoes onto the wagon. She continues, "I have to go back to work one of these days and I don't know how I'm going to concentrate on business. It kind of scares me."

"I had the same fears," I say. "But I worked a couple of nights at the hospital last week and it went better than I expected. It seemed once I got in my work environment I could do my job and forget about Phil for a while."

Sue's face pulls into a doubtful frown. "I hope I can." We finish loading up the vegetables and help Sue store them in the root cellar. The children have become bored with harvesting and are climbing about the swing set. Harry scowls at me whenever I look at him, which I know from experience means he's anxious to leave. I tell Sue we have to be going and we call out our good-byes to the children. I give Judie a long hug, thinking it will probably be Christmas before we see her again.

Sue fills a couple of bags with perishable vegetables and loads them into our car. "Thanks for your help. I'll call you," she says as we pull away.

Harry and I have barely enough energy left to unload the vegetables. We're not used to this kind of hard, physical work. After I pick up some fast food for our supper I strip off my muddy clothes, shower and get into my robe and slippers. I curl up on the end of the family room couch to watch TV and Harry lounges nearby in his favorite overstuffed chair.

I flip the channels and find an old movie about the life of Vincent Van Gogh starring Kirk Douglas and Anthony Quinn. As I watch I begin to see similarities between Philip's pensive personality and Van Gogh's creativity and ultra-sensitivity. I observe the traits that drove Van Gogh to suicide, and realize that some of the same characteristics were in Philip. The emotions stirred up by the troubled life of Van Gogh dredge up the old feelings I had during Philip's years of depression. Deeply saddened, I cry till I fall asleep.

Geri stops by in the morning accompanied by our friend, Therese. I begin talking to them about the

Van Gogh movie I watched, and the similarities I noticed between him and Philip. Geri looks embarrassed as I ramble on, and Therese looks distressed. They say hello to Harry and make a hurried departure.

The phone rings shortly after they leave. It's Harry's old school chum, George. We haven't seen George for a few years but he calls now and then to keep in touch. He and his wife Beth have just returned from vacationing in Florida and haven't heard about our loss. I tell him about Philip's recent death and fill him in on a few of the details about the how and where of his suicide.

George doesn't seem to know how to respond. We converse awkwardly for a few minutes. I know he likes to garden so I tell him about harvesting Philip's bountiful garden. I'm relieved when Harry comes to the phone to take up the conversation.

Just before lunch an attractive black woman comes to our door with a small boy in tow whom I estimate to be about five years old and probably her son. She announces herself as a Christian Witness and straight off asks if I read the Bible. "Yes," I tell her. She begins telling me what troubled times we are living in. "I know," I say bluntly. "My son killed himself two weeks ago." Normally I'm polite to these zealous Christians. I admire the time and effort they put into their faith. But today I feel irritated by her proselytizing and instinctively want to throw her off balance.

Her eyebrows shoot up and her mouth falls open,

leaving her speechless for a few moments. "Oh, I'm sorry," she says. "I don't know what to say. I never experienced anything like that."

"I hope you never do."

When she recovers her presence of mind, she rummages through her carryall and finds a pamphlet designed to console people who have lost a loved one. "Perhaps this will help," she says handing me the slim pamphlet. Forcing a smile, I accept it with my left hand while edging the door shut with my right. I toss it on the coffee table planning to read it later, and go out to the kitchen to make sandwiches for lunch. When we're done eating I stretch out on the couch to rest. I've been feeling very tired.

Upon awakening, I pick up the Christian woman's article. In spite of all the times I've been approached by these Witnesses, none have explained what they believe about life after death. According to this pamphlet, the dead remain in a state of oblivion, complete unawareness even more total than unconsciousness as we know it, until the end of the world. Then their bodies and souls return to life and are in some way indestructible but are exactly the same age as when they died; babies, teenagers, adults, senior citizens. "Strange theology," I think. "More than strange ... disturbing." I can't believe that babies are raised from the dead to go through growing up in eternity... or perhaps to remain babies. Are we older people going to grow older still? Or will we forever be heaven's seniors? The worst thing would be to believe that Philip will lie totally oblivious in his grave for centuries. I drop the pamphlet in the wastebasket, grateful that I don't have to believe that is what's happening to Philip.

It's October 12th, the day of Philip and Sue's thirteenth wedding anniversary. I picked out the perfect card for them months ago but can't send it now. I sit staring at the card for a long time, thinking about how they met, their long friendship, their wedding day. . .

When Philip is a freshman in high school he's in an art class with a pretty brown haired girl who has round, smiling eyes. They get together now and then during school time and at the end of the year she writes an affectionate message in his yearbook. "Dear Philly-Poo, Why did you have to be so good in art? Love Sue." They meet now and then throughout high school, and circulate with the same group of friends, but they never do any serious dating.

Once out of high school, after saving a little money from part-time jobs, Philip moved to a commune. We heard a lot about communes in the '60's as young people explored better ways of living. Philip's was an aging farmhouse on an abandoned farm in Cumberland, Wisconsin. I'd suspected him of monastic tendencies and his first letters from the commune point in that direction.

"Dear Mom,
　　It's starting to get cold up here so we're busy fixing up the house before it snows. There are six of us here . . . we're on a busy

schedule. Every morning we get up at six to a cold water scrub down, prayers, meditation, and spiritual exercises at dawn, then Tai Chi practice before breakfast followed by the day's work."

... "So, anyway, there is a lot of opportunity here for self improvement. These spiritual exercises are doing wonders and everybody is changing. I enjoy good, hard physical work. Looks like I might be here for quite a while, helping in my own small way to improve the world."

Near the end of summer we learn that Sue has moved up North to join the commune. We don't suspect a thing. At the end of August Phil writes to tell us the commune is disbanding and he's coming back to Milwaukee. We expect him to move back into our house. Not so. He and Sue move into the upper flat of a large triplex Judie and Jardo have bought on the East Side. It isn't long before Philip and Sue announce their wedding plans.

Thirteen years ago . . . if only we could relive those years, the last years of Philip's life. I would spend more time with them. Would do more to help them during those first difficult years, especially when the babies were born . . .

My friend, Margie, calls in the evening to ask how I'm feeling. "Terrible," I reply.
"What's the matter? Are you sick?"

"No. There's nothing physically wrong with me but I can't get my mind off Philip. Today was his thirteenth wedding anniversary."

"Oh, that must be rough. Is there anything I can do to help?"

I think about it for a few seconds. "No. I guess not." There doesn't seem to be much to talk about after that. It's becoming clear to me that others are forgetting about Philip's death and they feel uneasy when I keep bringing it up. I know I'm depressing and boring people and I resolve to keep my thoughts about him to myself.

❧ 6 ❧

Souvenirs

For the first time since I received it from the funeral director, I open the grocery bag containing the clothes Philip wore when he died. Carefully folded at the top, is his old red plaid flannel shirt. Beneath that I find a dirty, worn pair of jeans. I form a vivid mental picture of Philip walking toward me in these clothes. There's a red and white printed handkerchief in a pocket of the jeans. Wisps of dry grass scatter about me when I pull out the handkerchief. There are straws of the dry grass caught in his rolled up pants cuffs. He must have cut the grass the day he died. At the bottom of the bag are a pair of white cotton sweat socks, underpants, a brown leather belt twisted and stretched out of shape, and scuffed blue and white tennis shoes with paint spatters on them. The initials PJ are stitched into a design on the shoes. I wonder where he found shoes embroidered with his initials, PJ for Philip John.

The clothes smell strongly of gasoline. I breathe

in the unpleasant fumes. This was the odor Philip smelled during his final minutes of life. I gather the clothes into a bundle and hold them close. How good it would be to hold Philip in my arms, not just a bundle of his clothes. As I press them close I begin daydreaming about the times I held him, the time when he was part of me, when I felt the first stirrings of his body under my heart . . .

His gentle flutters assure me he's alive shortly before my second prenatal visit. My old family doctor says my pregnancy is proceeding normally, but he's not convinced my plans for natural childbirth are a wise choice. "You'll be putting yourself through a lot of needless trauma if you go through with this," he says sternly as he pages through the book I've given him.

"But I want to try it," I insist. "It couldn't be any worse than my last delivery. That was a terrible experience and I swore I'd never do it again."

"Mmm-hmmm," he says handing my book back to me. "I've read about natural childbirth. This Dr. Dick Read has been practicing it in England for a few years, but we don't know enough about its long term effects on mother and baby."

"You know, Dr. Read doesn't say it's painless. He calls it 'Childbirth Without Fear'. Being scared is what tenses your muscles and increases the pain."

"That sounds reasonable." I notice that the frown has left his forehead. "What's important is that we do what's best for you and the baby."

Five months later, after we've eaten our evening

meal, an unusual pressure in my lower abdomen and a sudden gush of water on the bathroom floor, prompt our immediate departure to the hospital. Feeling my abdomen caught in a vise-like grip I resist the urge to curl up into a tense ball. "Breathe deeply, slowly," I review the lessons I've been practicing for months.

At the hospital, prepped and ready for delivery, my masked doctor looks down into my face with serious eyes. "I have the anesthetic ready in case this gets to be too much for you."

The contractions tighten around my back and I feel the urge to bear down. The panting that I practiced as described in my book seemed silly, but now it feels natural and the only thing that keeps me from pushing when I'm not supposed to. After a few strong pushes the baby's head nears the outlet; the stretching and compressing of my caudal and peroneal nerve endings give me the sensation of being plunged into fire from the waist down. "This is pain," I admit letting out a low moan. I don't know how long I can stand this.

"I see the head," my doctor calls up from the foot of the delivery table. It's almost over. I can make it. I grab the hand grips for one last push and then relax. "It's a boy."

The sound of a new voice crying fills the room. The nurse places the wet sticky baby next to me and lets him squirm briefly in the crook of my arm. He frowns and screams, furious at being thrust out of his safe, warm nesting place. "My firstborn son," I think looking over his perfectly formed body in awe.

I could not have guessed then, the many ways in which this child would disrupt my deepest beliefs, would create and shatter my most cherished dreams.

Philip is a serious child right from the beginning. He watches us intently as we speak to him and knits his brows into a frown when his Grandparents 'kootchy koo' him. The night after he is baptized I tuck his curled, foot-long form into the six-year sized crib in the nursery, a minuscule bundle of a male person in whom the Holy Spirit now dwells.

"He belongs to you now, God. Please give him the best of every good thing." For the first time I feel my baby's separateness from me. He is his own person now, and God's, but still mine. Years of unknown potential stretch before him, and Harry and I are responsible for the molding. I feel overwhelmed by doubts about my own capabilities. "Dear God, this is too much for me. Please give me the strength and wisdom to raise him well. When I fail him, you take over. I trust in you for this."

. . . The acrid smell of gasoline irritating my nostrils brings me back to reality. I find myself hugging the bundle of clothes and rocking back and forth on the couch. I sit still for a long time looking at the clothes in my lap, fondling them, wondering what to do with them. I ought to throw them away. But I can't. Not just yet. I put the leather belt and the tennis shoes back into the bag, carry the other things down to the basement and put them in the washing machine. When they're clean and dry I fold them carefully and put them back into the bag. I roll the top down tightly and tape it shut. I lift the bag up to my closet shelf and push it toward the back. "I'll save them," I tell myself, "just a little longer."

I have tickets for a concert that evening and it turns out to be perfectly suited for my grief-damaged condition. The passionate music unlocks floods of emotion and I cry silently. The diffused colored lights and other-worldly sounds of one of the selections transports me into a fantasy of bodily resurrection and I imagine myself in a transformed world greeting Philip. The ecstasy peaks and then fades as the mystical music carries me into a reminiscence of the years when Philip abandoned his Christian faith in search of the truth that might be found in Eastern religions.

He is thirteen years old when he refuses to go to Sunday Mass with the family. He matter-of-factly announces that he doesn't believe in it any more. This is not the whiny protest of a child who would rather stay home and play. I knew how to deal with that. No amount of reasoning, punishing, bribing or threatening would convince him to set foot in our church.

I turn to our parish priest who conducts religious instruction for teenagers and he assures me that Philip isn't headed for damnation. "This questioning of the faith comes to many people at some time in their lives. Your son is just getting started younger than most of us. It isn't a bad or sinful thing to go through this, and God isn't going to condemn him for it."

Philip brings home books with unfamiliar titles: "Sidartha", "Concentration" by Mauni Sadhu, "Crest Jewel of Wisdom", "I Ching".

"What's 'I Ching'?" I ask. He invites me to read his books, and I do. It seems like a good idea to know where his head is traveling; if he should ever decide to discuss religion with me, I would have some answers ready.

I call Bill as soon as I return home from the concert, and tell him about the strong memories of Philip the music evoked in me. "The truth is, everything I see and hear makes me think about Philip. I think about him constantly." I tell him I've decided to stop talking to other people about him. "Everyone seems to have forgotten about him except me."

He agrees with me that others may be trying to forget Philip, attempting to get on with their lives. "You are still absorbing the reality of your loss."

"What other people don't realize is that I can never be the same person I was before Philip's death. For them it was a passing event, for me it will always be the tragic backdrop of my life." Bill does not refute this.

"You must always talk to me about Philip so you don't get bottled up inside. And keep writing about him in your journal. It's a good outlet for your emotions."

Hours of darkness tick by but sleep won't come. I try to pray, but the usual question surfaces. "How could you let this happen to Philip?" The anger in my soul boils up and over. I'm filled with a terrible rage. I jerk out of bed and walk into our guest room, the same room that had been the nursery many years ago. Alone in the darkened room, I stand in the exact spot where, thirty-three years earlier, I stood in awe looking down into the oversized crib at the tiny baptized person named Philip John. Deep wrenching sobs begin to shake my body. "God!" I cry out. "I asked you to help me take care of him that day he was baptized. I kept on asking you all the years he was growing up. I told you I couldn't do it alone. I entrusted him to your care. You have betrayed me, abandoned me." I close the nursery door so I don't wake up Harry. "God!" I shout. "How could you let his life end so cruelly? How could you do this to him? I trusted you. We all trusted you."

Then somehow, without making a sound I scream at God. Looking up to heaven I send up silent, furious screams that rip up from the depths of my soul and tear through the corners of the universe till I am sure they have pierced the heart of God. I scream at Him again and again. "Why did you do this to Philip?" I demand to know. "Why? Why?" When my fury is exhausted I walk silently to my bed and fall down into a deep sleep.

God didn't strike me dead as I supposed He might. I wake up peacefully, lazily, for the first time in weeks. As the day ripens I discover that I can pray. Prayer comes easily. I feel God's loving presence, as in the old days before grief.

➤➤ 7 ◀◀

Steel Boy

I sit down with my stationery, surrounded by memorial cards, notes of sympathy, cards that had been attached to flowers or food, and spend the day writing thank you notes. I read and reread the sentiments Philip's friends express about his goodness to them, his caring, and how much they are going to miss him. I cry with each letter, with each friend, and write my notes through blurry eyes.

One note begins, "I know exactly what you're going through. I'll give you some time to tie up your loose ends and then we'll get together for a long talk. Love, Sally"

Ordinarily I'd bristle at someone who presumes to know my suffering. But not Sally. Her teenage daughter took the same life escape route as Philip— a car in a garage with a motor running, five years ago. Now she tells me she feels like a normal human being again. How in hell did she get through it? Yes, I need to talk to Sally.

By the end of the day my sinuses are clogged

from crying; my throat feels tight and sore. While Harry sips on his before dinner martini, I fix myself a brandy on ice. At first the cold liquid soothes my throat and I feel better, but within fifteen minutes my arms and legs feel weighted down, and my head gets woozy. I manage to finish making dinner and eat a few bites before lying down on the couch. The outer world retreats as my body relaxes, but inside, in the center of my being, I'm acutely aware of my broken heart.

When my head clears I call Bill and tell him about the exhausting day I had reading and replying to the beautiful words Philip's friends wrote about him. "He was always doing kind things for others. That was his main goal in life, to make the world better for others. That's mostly what he prayed for."

"Don't start fantasizing about him and making him a saint now that he's dead." His harsh reply feels like a physical blow, but he goes on. "He had his faults, some very serious ones. Pride and stubbornness kept him closed in upon himself. He wouldn't express his inner struggles to others. He didn't believe anyone could help him. In his pain and sickness he made a terrible mistake in taking his own life. God allowed Philip to kill himself, but that's not what God wanted for him. Suicide is never the right solution to problems."

I'm hurt and angered by his reply. I pause a few seconds attempting to harness my feelings. When I answer my words sound frigid. "Okay, Bill. I'll think about that. Goodbye."

I can't fall asleep. Bill's harsh words continue to

irritate me, but I begin to realize that I have treasured Philip's finer qualities and interred the disagreeable ones with his bones. He was stubborn. Immovable stubbornness was the dark side of his determined will. Even as a toddler he seemed ready to suffer all manner of discomforts rather than give in to others.

The full strength of his stubborn will emerged when he was nine years old. A few months into the first semester of fourth grade, he comes home after school, drops his books on the kitchen table and makes a quiet complaint. "My teacher is a big bully."

I never heard him refer to a teacher in this manner. "Why do you say that?"

"He makes fun of us when we make a mistake."

"That doesn't sound like a good thing for a teacher to do. Do you try to do your best in school?" A superficial question. I know he does. He always did.

He nods silently.

"Try to be nice to him. School's just started. Maybe he hasn't been teaching very long. Give him a chance to improve."

Philip looks gloomy as he plods off to school each morning, but I hear no more complaints about his teacher. At the end of the first semester, my "A" student's report card surprises me. Not only a 'C's and D's' but a note from his teacher, Mr. Lane, complaining about his deportment. When I question Philip he says. "I can't help it. Mr. Lane is mean and he's dumb."

The school principal is still in her office and

listens patiently to my report on Philip's unusually bad grades due to his supposedly bad teacher. "Mr. Lane is new to our school this year," she explains. As you know, we no longer have enough teaching sisters to cover all of our grades. I've been made aware that Mr. Lane's teaching methods are a bit unusual. I've discussed this with him and we are taking steps to correct the discrepancies. Philip is a good student. I'm sure if he will try to cooperate with Mr. Lane he will do just fine."

I relay her message to Philip. "Hmmmph!" he says shooting me a disgusted look. Unfortunately I rely on the Sister Superior's judgment rather than on his. I'm still naive enough to believe the old adage from my school days. "The teacher is always right".

On a rainy day near the end of March, Philip comes home from school with a great armload of books. I catch a glimpse of him trudging up the back walk. He carries his books to the back fence where the trash cans are lined up, nudges open the nearest can, and drops his books into it.

"Philip! What are you doing? You're going to need those books."

"No. I'm never going to school again."

"Philip! You're only ten years old." My voice rises to a nasty shrieking pitch. "You have to go to school. You have a lot more to learn."

"I'll stay home and read. I already learned enough stuff at school." My brain latently picks up on the seriousness of Philip's school problems.

I reach Sister Superior and load her with a detailed account of Philip's continuing school problems. She apologizes. "Please send Philip to school and I'll arrange for his transfer to another classroom."

Too late! No amount of reasoning, coaxing, threatening, or force that Harry and I conjure up, makes Philip return to school.

I know Philip's problem is not physical but, in desperation, I take him to our family doctor. Our doctor runs a few lab tests and examines him but the only thing he comes up with is, perhaps Philip is a little underweight. "I know a good child psychologist who might be able to help him." I feel humiliated admitting that Philip needs to see a psychologist. I'm not long out of the era that connected a stigma of failure with needing therapy to handle one's problems. But, what else can we do? I set up the appointment.

As Harry and I squirm uneasily in our waiting room chairs, the psychologist consults privately with Philip. After a full hour the two of them emerge smiling. "There's nothing wrong with Philip," he assures us. "He's a sensitive child who's had some very negative experiences this past school year. The teacher in question may know his subject material, but he certainly doesn't understand how to teach children. He was the biggest problem for Phil."

"In addition to that, as you are probably aware, Philip doesn't like the rough and tumble games some of the other boys play. That's perfectly normal. Not all of us do. The problem is that some of them have been calling him a 'sissy'. As I told Phil, I see many boys in my office who have the same problem." He smiles down at Philip and reaches over to give him a hug. Philip looks up at him with a smile. I'm amazed to see how rapidly the therapist has gained rapport with my usually shy, reticent child. "Phil found out that children can be very cruel and, what is worse, so can adults. But, as I explained to him, none of us can go around making the world be nice to him. He has to learn to cope."

"Yes." I see Harry nodding his head with a far away look in his eyes. "I remember running into the same problems as a boy. It's not easy being a kid . . . Well," he focuses his eyes on the psychologist, "will Philip go back to school now?"

"At this point I would suggest a change of environment. So many unpleasant things have happened to Philip this year, it would be impossible to erase that negative image for quite some time. I would recommend a fresh start in a different school."

With only a short time left in the school year, we decide to let Philip stay home and read. We make plans to enroll him in the local public grade school in the Fall. I feel uneasy about it because we had planned to send all the children to Catholic grade and high schools. Will his religious education suffer? Probably. But, as things stand, we've no other choice.

His new school comes equipped with a full complement of experienced teachers and a more structured environment that controls teasing and bullying. As the new school year unfolds, Harry and

I watch Philip grow in wisdom and self-esteem.

I lie motionless while the dawn lightens my bedroom window shade. Reflections of Philip's childhood continue to rise up out of the closets of my memory. I'm unable to sleep but feel too tired to get up. In this state of torpor I begin to sense that Philip is standing next to me. I feel his presence as strongly as if he has walked in through the bedroom door. His presence, or spirit, bends down to embrace me, and I hold him to myself for a long time. I tell him how much I love him and how much I miss him.

In a mystical way I hear his answering words. He assures me that he knows all the things I want to tell him because he is very close to me. He loves me and doesn't want me to cry anymore. I whisper his name aloud several times and each time an intense wave of happiness washes through me. Before his presence fades I am filled with joy

I rise in eager anticipation of the new day—my first happy day since Philip died. His bliss, his love, his nearness follow me and I find I can think and talk about him without sadness. Harry and I stop in to visit Memere and we find her crying about Philip. "Don't cry Mem," I tell her. "He is close to us and we'll see him again in heaven."

"Yes. I know he's there. He did so many kind things for me. After Pepere died I told Phil I didn't know who would take care of me when I became too old to live alone. He said right away, 'You can come and live with us, Mem.' I never knew anyone as sensitive and dear as Phil."

That evening I phone Bill to tell him about my visit from Philip "I remember, after my Dad died, my mother told me about him coming to her one night. I assumed she was just dreaming. But this was too real… much more powerful than a dream."

"In my years of counseling I've heard this quite a few times from those who are newly bereaved. We aren't sure if these are mystical encounters or dreams. I tend to believe they are more than just dreams, because people who report them say they are. We all have dreams and we know what they're like. On awakening we realize they are dreams. But this experience is never interpreted as a dream by those who encounter it, only by psychologists who feel compelled to put scientific tags on the whole human psyche. One thing is certain, they are tremendously beneficial in healing grief."

I go to bed that night feeling happy, thinking that I am done with grieving. A bizarre dream warns me that this is not what's in store for me.

In my dream all of our children are living at home again, including Jardo, and we are busy assembling our camping gear in preparation for a vacation trip. An evil man who looks like Edward G. Robinson forces his way into our house and takes over one of our second floor bedrooms. He has a nuclear bomb in his satchel and tells us he is planning to blow up a quarter of a million people. He comes into the kitchen to eat with us and tells us about his plan. When he sits down at the kitchen table with his back to me I quietly take a rolling pin out of the drawer, sneak up behind him and begin hitting him on the head with all my might. I want to kill him but no matter how many times I hit him I know he is only stunned.

I hurry into our back hall looking for a rope to tie him to the chair, but all I can find is Penny's dog chain. Grabbing it quickly I return to the kitchen but the evil man is gone. "Why did you let him get away?" I ask the others angrily. "He's dangerous." They look apologetic and distressed, but they don't speak. The man has gone back upstairs. Then Jardo gets up and goes after him and I hear them talking. Jardo is trying to reason with him.

I wake up periodically during the night tossing about in my nightmare. Always, when I fall back to sleep, the evil man is lurking in the background. Just before morning I dream of hurrying everyone to finish with the packing so we can leave on our camping trip and get away from him.

This dream will not leave my memory during the days that follow. It pushes into my thoughts weighting me with a sense of foreboding. I become convinced that the evil man is the specter of grief crouching in hidden places ready to destroy us without warning. I know I will not be able to eradicate this evil, even if I try with all my might. I want to take the whole family away, to a place where there is no grief.

I make an entry in my journal. It's a letter to Philip.

"Dear Philip,

I know you are near and don't want me to grieve anymore, but there will always be the sadness of your tragic end. The world has suffered a great loss because you are not in it to champion the causes of peace, simplicity of life, and your special crusade of bread for the poor. We need you Philip. If only there had been some way we could help you overcome your depression. Then we could have kept you with us. I miss you very much."

Harry watches me puttering around the kitchen as I prepare the evening meal and he asks me if I would like a brandy. "You look like you're having a hard day."

"I am. Sure, I'll take one. Maybe it will numb the pain." I take a sip of the icy liquid. "It was tough for Philip. He could never drink this stuff because he was an alcoholic. He had to face his pain stone sober." Harry doesn't answer. He is sipping on brandy too. "Remember how stubborn Phil could be?" The brandy loosens my verbal inhibitions and I ramble on. "When he made up his mind to something, nothing could make him change it. That stubbornness combined with the rest of his pensive traits was probably what made his life extremely difficult . . . like Father Gerard said; Phil wouldn't change his idealistic attitudes, but he couldn't bear to live with them either."

"Probably wasn't much we could have said or

done to help him," Harry concludes.

"I keep trying to figure out ways we might have saved him. Sue and I never stopped praying for him. I knew he had problems, but I never dreamed they were that severe. I remember the week before he died thinking about him and feeling I should call and see how he was doing. I was busy that week over at the new house, working in the attic. I didn't get around to calling. How I wish now I would have called him. Maybe my interest in his well being would have made the difference. Maybe he would have hung on to life. Maybe . . maybe . . I'll never know now, will I? God! How I wish I would have called him."

"It doesn't help to keep thinking about it. Just forget it."

I can't forget it. Even in my fuzzed up brandy world the remorse gnaws inside me. Somehow I get through dinner and without cleaning up the dishes I go to my room to rest. I feel crushed . . . beaten. I turn to the only one who knows the extent of my misery, and He is there. My angry outburst at Him the other night has dissolved the barrier between us. "God, I'm sorry I didn't call Philip that last week. I'm sorry if it's my fault he died. I'm sorry for my everlasting busy-ness that keeps me from doing the things that really matter. What can I do about it now? Tell you I'm sorry? Tell Philip I'm sorry? Just live with this pain and pray for mercy and healing? Help me to live with this pain, this guilt, and I promise to be more attentive to ways I can help others."

As soon as I feel sober enough to speak clearly, I call Bill to tell him how guilty I feel about not calling Philip the week before he died. "Maybe my caring about him would have made him want to live."

Bill senses the extremity of my distress and his words come gently. "That's not true. Even if you called him it would have done no good." The tenderness in his voice feels like a soothing balm flowing in to cover my wounds. "Your trying to help may even have hastened his suicide by making him feel incompetent to handle his own life." He pauses to let this truth sink in. "In any case, he would have done it no matter what you said to him. Then you would have been wondering what you said that made him kill himself."

The truth of his words penetrates instantly. "You're right. I would have gone over that conversation a hundred times wondering what I said that made him kill himself."

"There was absolutely nothing you could have said or done that would have prevented this. He had drawn more and more into his shell. He turned everything into a reason to kill himself. Even if you had handed him a million dollars and told him he could quit his job and buy the farm of his dreams, it would have done no good."

"Not even the farmland? . . . I wonder . . " Owning his own farm was his lifetime dream.

"Not even that," Bill states firmly.

"It's hard for me to comprehend that."

"That's because you've never had that kind of depression. You've never been suicidal. Remember, he had a suicide contract with his psychiatrist and he broke that too." Philip had signed an agreement with his doctor saying he would not take his own life before contacting her.

"That's right. I forgot about that." My breath comes easier with the burden of guilt lifting off my chest. I decide to press on with one other problem I've been mulling over. "Another thing's been bothering me. God had to know about Philip's suicide all along, but he never gave me the slightest clue it would happen."

"To do that would have been to violate free will, both yours and Philip's. Philip did not want you to know about his plans. God will not violate our free will."

"Then God was as helpless as I was to prevent this?"

"That's right. God controls all of creation. He can alter the course of natural events. But, he will never force His will on His human creatures."

"But God must have felt Philip's increasing torment those years before he died."

"Jesus, on the cross, felt the suffering of every person that ever lived. When He said 'I thirst' He wanted more love and more suffering." There is a long pause while he waits for my reply. I've been told this truth countless numbers of times in church, and thought I believed it. Now, the reality of all that it implies seems too incredible to absorb.

"I can't comprehend that much love. Even though it makes Him suffer, He won't force us to stop our self destruction?"

"No!"

I pause to let his words sink in before I reply. "You've given me a lot to think about, Bill. I feel better." He makes me promise to call if anything else comes up

"I'm going to stop in the chapel this morning," I say to Judy, the nurse I've worked with through the night shift, as we walk toward the employee exit. I work full time night shift at the hospital again—ten-hour shifts, four times a week.

The new chapel is small with benches for about twenty worshipers, and has the discomforting stark look of Danish modern. It's empty this morning. I kneel in a back pew and as I raise my eyes to the altar I'm at once filled with a combination of peace, joy, and exaltation. I know with certainty that Jesus has suffered this grief with me, and has suffered with Philip in his long struggle with depression. And not only that, Jesus silently assures me He has suffered enough to make up for Philip's lack of faith, for his painful mental illness that blinded him to the truth, and for the mistake he made in taking his own life. His redeeming life and crucifixion have turned around Philip's weakness—turned it into a resurrection union with God. "Behold, I make all things new!" His words sing through me.

For days I'm filled with gratitude for God's love, and especially for Philip's redemption. I feel a kinship with all the people in the world struggling with sin and sorrow. I feel close to my loved ones who have gone on ahead of Phil; to my mother and father, to Pepere, and to my grandmother.

Then I think of Christ's mother, Mary. My God! What if she had said "no" to his birth? I thank her for all the times she said 'Yes' to what God willed for her. "She stood beneath his cross and, with Him, willed His death." Willed his pain; willed his physical separation from her; willed annihilation of a mother's hopes and dreams for her child. Having lost my son in such a cruel way, I know some of the anguish that "yes" had cost her.

❊ 8 ❊

Leftovers

Sue calls to ask for my help. "I'll be going through Phil's things on Saturday morning. It'd be easier with you here, and there are some clothes and hunting gear that maybe your other boys can use."

"Just a minute, I'll check my work schedule." Luckily I'm off Friday night. "Sure, I'll come to help. How about nine-thirty?"

"Fine, we'll be up by then. I haven't been sleeping well anyway. I wake up too early and start going over all this stuff about Phil. I miss him so much."

"I can imagine. You shared your life with him more closely than the rest of us for the last fourteen years. I wasn't with him as much as you were, but I miss him terribly now that he's gone. I think about him all the time. I keep calling Bill to ask him about these crazy things that go through my head." I tell her about my conversations with Bill. She tells me she's been having some of the same worries.

We talk for forty-five minutes. I share the

inspirations I received in the chapel after work, and she tells me about some insights she's come upon through prayer. It's a relief to know someone who needs to talk about Philip.

Sue is clearing out Philip's dresser when I arrive. She has some of his things sorted out on their waterbed. I look over the assortment of clothes, most of which I've never seen. "If anyone would have asked me I'd have told them Phil had three flannel shirts and a couple pairs of jeans. Here he's got a whole closet full of shirts and trousers… and an entire dresser with T-shirts and sweaters."

"I know. He hardly ever wore these things. Some of them are brand new. Most of them he got for birthday and Christmas presents. He never wanted to wear anything but his plaid shirts and jeans. I used to get mad at him and want him to dress up. He looked so handsome when he dressed up, especially in his new suit."

"He did look fine in that. I always thought he was handsome." I form a mental image of him in his suit and hold onto it as we work. "Look! Here's the wedding shirt you made for him with the Yin Yang symbol embroidered on it."

Sue's eyes mist over recalling the memories of that day. "I'm going to save that." Not wishing to disturb her reverie we work for a while in the silence of remembering.

"I love these T-shirts," I say at last, unable to contain my delight. "This one is my favorite." I hold up a shirt with a picture of Uncle Sam, his finger pointing toward me. I saw plenty of pictures like this on recruiting posters during World War II, and even a few during Vietnam. This one has a slightly different message. 'Join the Navy and See the World' is printed under Uncle Sam, followed by 'Meet Exotic People and Kill Them'.

Sue laughs. "He wore that one to a reception for our new pastor at church. I was so embarrassed. It turned out all right though. The pastor was a war protester too and he got a big kick out of it." Her smile fades quickly retracing lines of sorrow about her eyes and mouth. "Phil always liked to make a statement with his shirts."

"Phil tried to change the world in every way he could, didn't he?"

"Yes. I think that was part of his problem. He never lost that idealism we had in the old 'Nam' days. He kept writing to his congressmen as long as I knew him about issues of non-violence and justice. Remind me to show you the copies of the letters and magazine articles he saved."

"No wonder he felt depressed. No matter how hard we work and pray the world seems to keep going downhill." My thoughts fill with fond memories of the altruism of the sixties. It was the noblest era I'd seen in my lifetime. I felt depressed when it fizzled out. "I'll bet it bothered Philip that so many of his old buddies lost interest in the struggle once they got involved in making a living for their families."

"Yes, and he got mad at me for not going with him to the 'Human Concerns Committee' and

'Bread for the Poor' meetings. I just couldn't though, and I told him so. I work all day at my job trying to salvage peoples' lives. I need to relax in the evening and think about something else. He used to get frustrated at the lack of response he'd get from a lot of people."

"He asked me to come out a couple of times to help. I was always too busy. I feel terrible about it now. I wish I would have done more to help him."

"You? You have enough things to keep you busy where you are . . I know what you mean though. I keep wondering if I did the right thing, if I should have helped him more."

We work quietly for a while. I think about Philip's life, his needs. Would he still be alive if we had done more for him? More with him? I don't know.

Sue puts some of the T-shirts and socks aside for Josh. "He's growing so fast. These things will fit him soon. He likes to wear oversized shirts. It seems to be the style now." Josh has just turned twelve, entering that age of rigid peer conformity.

Sue hangs the embroidered wedding shirt at the back of Philip's closet along with a few other clothes that hold special memories of their life together. The rest we pack in grocery bags and boxes, some for me to take home, and some for her to take to church.

"Would you mind helping me sort through his books and papers now? He saved all the books and notes from his classes. He always told me not to throw anything out because he might need to look something up."

I look through the ponderous books on organic and analytic chemistry, and the indecipherable notes that accompany them. Sue sees me shaking my head in awe and says, "He was really smart. I used to think he was too smart. It seems the most intelligent people have the hardest time getting along in this world. Phil wanted to figure everything out. He wasn't satisfied until he did."

She walks over to their bookcase and points at the rows of hard cover and paperback books. "Look at all these books he read on philosophy and psychology. He got me to read a lot of them." She picks out a book here and there, and stacks them on one edge of the shelf. "I'm going to save some of these that I haven't read yet."

I begin packing others in neat rows, checking out the titles as I do so. I recognize some of the books on Eastern religions he'd read during his years of searching for the perfect way. "Phil had a great library here. With all this knowledge you'd think he could have found the way to live a happy life." I cast a questioning look at Sue.

"You'd think so." She raises her hands in a futile gesture. "Toward the end he gave up trying. For about the last six months he started concentrating on pleasure. He just wanted to have fun. That's when he started drinking again." Her face contorts with the painful memory.

"We noticed he was more cheerful last summer. Not one of us suspected he'd gone back to drinking. I thought he was cured of his depression." I fight hard to keep back the tears so I can keep packing the books. When we finish with them we sit down on the bed to rest. Sue's eyes are wet. She lifts a tissue to her face to absorb the droplets forming on her lashes.

"I got mad at him when I found out he was drinking. He said he just wanted to drink a little bit so he wouldn't feel so depressed. Once he started though, he could never stop. Then he got even more depressed because he couldn't control his drinking. I started feeling depressed myself and I could tell it was bothering the kids." She shakes her head as if trying to undo what happened next.

"We had a long discussion the night before he died. I told him I couldn't live with him if he kept drinking. Alcohol was like an evil force that came between us. I said he should go back for inpatient treatment again. 'What's the use?' he asked. 'I already tried that and it didn't make me feel any better.'" She looks up at me in bewilderment as she continues. "I've thought a lot about that confrontation since he died. I wonder how much it contributed to his suicide."

I nod my head. She's shouldering the blame for Philip's death just as I am. "You said what you thought was right at the time," I say, repeating the advice I've been giving to myself.

"I guess so. I had to take a stand on his drinking problem. We couldn't go on the way things were. I wish now I would have taken him right in to the treatment center in the morning. I thought about it."

"It might have kept him alive, at least for a while.

But from what you've said it doesn't sound as though he would have gone."

"I don't know. I think he would have gone if I insisted. I just don't know. I keep thinking about that night... going over the things we said . . ."

The boxes of Philip's clothes, hunting gear, bits and pieces of his life, are still piled by our living room door, ready to be divided among his brothers. They remind me of how much I long for the physical presence of my dead son. The sharp pain of grief in my heart is being replaced by a dull ache of sorrow filled with memories of the sight and sound of Philip. Just as Sue is doing, I search for ways that I might have saved him, go over conversations I might have had with him...words that would have made him want to live. I write a letter to him in my journal:

My Dearest Philip,

I'm sure you never dreamed that your death would make so many of us grieve. I'm sure you never believed that we loved you this much. I wish I would have told you that I love you. Now, in spirit, I hold you tenderly in my arms and feel the joy and the healing you are receiving from God. Now you know that your depression and pain were all a mistake. Products of a too tender heart, a mind full of impossible ideals. . . perhaps goaded from below by uneasy phantoms of your subconscious. If I was the cause of some of those phantoms, I'm sorry. And the imperfections of your body inherited from Dad and me, that made you prone to alcoholism... some imbalance of endorphins or electrolytes... all a fluke of anatomy. Again, I'm sorry.

All mistakes. Nothing more. If you had ever asked me I would have told you so. But I suppose you wouldn't have believed me. Your happiness was buried under layer upon layer of physical and psychological mistakes. You can see now that most of the happiness in the world is buried under tons of mistakes. Some day God will come and transform the world by digging us out. Then we will all be together in love and happiness. I've been thinking more and more of that day. Then I will see you again. We all miss you very much.

"This one looks like it's from Peter," Harry pulls an envelope from the stack of letters he's brought in from the mailbox. He hands it to me to read. It's dated October 24th.

"We're all back at work now and trying to get our minds on what we're supposed to be doing. Eddie didn't seem quite himself after we got back from Philip's funeral. It must be hard for a six year old to figure out why someone goes away and can never come back. Jill and I sat down and talked with him about it, and we're giving him some extra attention these days."

"Jim and his wife Cathy came over

and expressed their regrets that they couldn't come to Milwaukee for the funeral. Jim and I talked a long time about Phil. I never realized how well Jim got to know Phil during our high school years. Jim told me about the long discussions they had. He said Philip read so much he could discuss just about any topic at great length . . called him a 'Renaissance Man'. Guess I kind of took Phil for granted. Sometimes we hung out together but I never really talked to him that much."

"Jim told me about the time he walked into our bedroom (that was when Phil and I shared the same room) and saw Phil sitting at the desk staring at the big wall clock which he had taken down and propped up in front of him. 'I watched him for a while and he didn't move,' said Jim. 'When I asked him what he was doing he said, "I'm trying to find out how long an hour is." That really blew my mind. I went home and tried the same thing myself. I only lasted ten minutes.'"

"The people in my department got together and sent a plant to you and the family. You should have gotten it by now. They've been great and, as you know, I took a lot of extra time off to come to Milwaukee, but nobody's complaining."

"Hope you and Dad are okay. Love, Peter."

We receive the plant Peter wrote about. It's a large broad-leaf cactus with sharp spines along the outer edges of the leaves, about three feet tall from the base of the pot to the top of the tallest leaf. A thick stalk rises from the center topped by a fire-red, spear-shaped flower. The blossom is five inches long and is edged with feathery wheat-colored sprays. It looks like a space odyssey creation. The directions that come with it say that it blooms only once in its lifetime, then slowly withers and dies. But before it dies it sends up a new plant called a 'pup' from its roots. As we watch it go through its life and death cycle I think about how appropriate a gift it is as a remembrance of Philip.

The day before Halloween we take care of Josh and Sarah for the morning. They're well-behaved children and we enjoy their company. Harry and I play monopoly with them, and then we go out to rake leaves. Watching them play with leaves opens a scene in my memory from that Fall day Philip and I walked with them through the treatment center grounds. After the leaves are piled in the gutter we take the children to visit Memere. She's pleased to see them. She fusses over them, stuffing them with candy and cookies.

During our visit we are careful not to talk about Philip because we want the children to have a happy day. I begin to notice a heavy depressed feeling pushing down on me; a different sensation than the usual ache in my chest. I wrap a cloak of gayety and smiles around myself and hang on tight.

We take Josh and Sarah to see our fantastic pumpkin exhibit. Every Halloween our village displays hundreds of carved pumpkins in a small park near the library. Most of the carving is done by one of the residents who has a great talent with pumpkins. Josh and Sarah look delighted as they walk about the display examining the carvings. "Wow! says Josh."

'I didn't know there could be hundreds of ways to carve a pumpkin!" says Sarah.. Their enthusiasm assures me they're having a good time.

Sue picks them up during her lunch hour and takes them to visit her mother. After they leave I say to Harry, "I don't know what's the matter with me. All the while they were here I had a heavy, sad feeling. I tried not to let it show."

"I guess you hid it. I didn't notice you were sad."

"That's good. I didn't want the kids to feel it. I'm not sure what the sadness is about. Maybe it's just that they remind me of Philip. Or maybe I'm sad because his suicide left them without a father." The depression hangs on to me the rest of the day. My heart feels like a rock.

I call Bill in the evening to tell him about it.

"You have a lot of repressed anger inside," he tells me.

"But what am I angry about? Am I angry at Philip for leaving his children?"

"Yes, and you're not able to let it out. Maybe you should see a psychologist; one who is good at dealing with repressed anger." He gives me the name of a reliable specialist in this field and I agree to contact her.

When I call to make an appointment with her I'm disappointed to learn that she doesn't accept my medical insurance. Her fee is very high, more than I can pay at this time. I ask Bill if he knows of anyone else. "Not off hand. I'll check some other sources. You've got to be very careful about psychologists when you're grieving like this. You're extremely vulnerable. I've seen some grief stricken people totally messed up by the wrong psychologist."

I call Sue at work to see if she can recommend someone. Her job as a social worker puts her in touch with people in that field.

"I don't know of any individual who does that specifically, but here's something that might help. It's a group that meets monthly called 'Survivors of Suicide'. It's usually helpful to get together with people who've gone through the same thing, and find out how they're working out their problems. I'm thinking of going to the group meetings myself."

I call the number Sue gives me and talk to the woman who organized the group. "My husband took his own life seventeen years ago and I realized I had a great need to talk about it. I got in touch with other people I heard about, whose loved ones had committed suicide. We began meeting in my home once a month. The group became so large, we now use the conference room in a health center for our meeting."

"Do I have to make an appointment or fill out anything if I decide to come?"

"Oh, no. It's not formal at all. There are no dues

or anything like that. Just come if you feel like it." I write down the address and the date of the next meeting. It will be held a few days after Thanksgiving.

I tell Harry and the children about the group. "It's open to anyone, if you want to come with me."

The invitation sparks an enthusiastic reply from Geri. "I'll go with you, Mom." Cathy and Peggy think it might be a good idea. They'll let me know. Harry gives me a flat 'no', and Mike is not interested. When the time for the meeting comes, Geri and I go together. Sue has joined a group that meets closer to her home.

There are about twenty-five people sitting at tables grouped together in a circle. We take turns introducing ourselves and tell briefly about the suicide that has brought us here. One of the participants is a father whose son killed himself three days ago. The boy was in an alcoholic treatment center when he took his own life. He used a plastic bag from a trash can to smother himself. I immediately think of Sue wishing she had taken Philip in for treatment the morning of his suicide. I see now that if a person is determined to end his life there's no way to stop him. I must tell her about this.

Some of the people talk a lot and express themselves freely; others are quiet. The group leader is skillful in drawing out each one's story. A couple my age tells about their son who shot himself two years ago. "We miss him so terribly," his father says. "It's especially hard during hunting season. We always went hunting together."

I picture Harry's gloomy return from deer hunting on Jardo's farm last weekend. He and Philip, together with Chris and Frank, have been hunting there since Judie and Jardo bought the farm ten years ago. "It was pretty bad," Harry said coming in the front door and plopping his gear down on the living room floor. "I don't think I'm going hunting anymore."

A young girl speaks at great length about her mother's suicide four years earlier. She reads a poem she's written about how it happened. Her eyes are red and swollen. She chokes back the tears as she reads. She blames her Dad and other family members for not helping her mother.

One older woman is angry. She says she hates life. She doesn't trust herself or anyone else since her husband committed suicide. She threatens to kill herself. During her interchange with the group leader I learn that she has been coming to these meetings and threatening suicide for several years. Stuck in her paranoia, she can't find a way out.

All of the suicides and the grief they have engendered sound heartbreakingly sad. One of the stories chills me with its cruelty. An attractive young woman whose husband killed himself just one week earlier, states that the man's family has threatened and verbally abused her since it happened. She is shaking uncontrollably as she tells us that the marriage wasn't working out. That they'd been separated for a month before his death. "They keep telling me it's my fault. Some of them won't speak to me at all."

At the end of the session the leader introduces a professional therapist who is available for individual counseling. The young widow immediately goes over to speak to him. I copy his name and phone number in case I decide to call him. There are free therapeutic pamphlets and books on a table. Geri and I gather up a few things to read.

"I'm amazed to find out how many people have a relative who committed suicide," says Geri during the drive home.

"I am too. I guess it's something people don't normally talk about. There must be hundreds of us walking around out here who have had this terrible experience."

"Yes. And what really shakes me up is that they're still talking about it and crying years later. I can't imagine myself crying and being sad for such a long time," she adds.

"I can't either. I couldn't stand to have these painful feelings for years and years."

❊ 9 ❊

Love Rock

A few days later, on a cold drizzly weekend, Harry and I help Sue and the children move to a new house. She must leave their newly remodeled cottage at the retreat house now that Philip is no longer the caretaker. We share many tears as we part with the home he has helped to build: Sue's much loved sewing room, their bountiful garden, the little touches of his productive hands that must be left behind. He'd had a comfortable life insurance policy, enough for Sue's down payment on a spacious house a few miles from Saint Francis Cemetery. From her new front window I see the majestic spires of Holy Hill church reaching up into heavy clouds.

"It's a good thing I'm moving," Sue says when we have a minute to sit down and rest. "I was nervous living alone with the kids after that article in our local newspaper."

"What article?"

"I thought I told you. I'm getting so forgetful."

She fishes a small newspaper out of an untidy stack on the kitchen table and hands it to me.

My mouth falls open as I read the headline. "LOCAL MAN'S DEATH RULED A SUICIDE. Philip Olive of," . . to my dismay the complete address is given, "was found overcome by carbon monoxide in the garage near his house on September 25th. A suicide note was found inside his home shortly after his body was discovered . . ."

"A suicide note? I didn't know he left a note!"

"I didn't either till I read it in the paper. The sheriff found the note on the kitchen table under a rock when he searched the house before I got home that day. They never even told me about it. You can imagine how furious I was. I drove right to the station and demanded to have it back."

"God, Sue. I can't believe they'd do such a crummy thing . . . and not even tell you about it. What did the note say?"

"I have it here." She hands me a crumpled four by four slip that had been torn from a note pad. I recognize Philip's small irregular printing. 'Dear Sue, Josh, and Sarah, I love you very much. I will always love you. I'm sorry to disappoint you like this. Love, Phil.'

I smooth my fingers over his last penciled words. Anger and grief vie for possession of my emotions.

Sue continues filling me in on the rest of the tacky details. "They didn't want to give this to me. . . said it was evidence. They tried to give me a Xerox copy. I said I wouldn't leave without the original. They couldn't understand why I was so upset. 'This makes a big difference to me.' I told them. 'He thought of us. He loves me. You had no right to take this away, and not even tell me about it. I had to read it in the paper.' Then I yelled at them for letting the newspaper print my name and address, with me living out in the country all alone with the kids. That could have been dangerous."

"Very dangerous. What a botched up mess. They made this tragedy worse than it already was. And Sue, what if you didn't happen to read that paper? You'd never know his last words to you and the kids." Sue's mouth is set in a grim line, the anger flashing from her eyes. "Anyway, in this case I'm glad you're moving into a new house. It'll be safer."

"How can we possibly celebrate Christmas this year? None of us feels like putting up a tree or exchanging presents." Bill turns a sympathetic gaze on me. He understands perfectly how I feel. His own mother is in a hospice dying of lung cancer.

"We both have to celebrate Christmas this year. You for your family, and I for my Dad and all my friends who would have nowhere else to go for the holidays. It's important for us to keep up all of our usual holiday traditions." I guess he's right. Maybe my family does need to have Christmas as usual this year. I wonder how I'll get through it.

I push myself around the shopping malls selecting the gifts I need, feeling out of place amid the bright Christmas trimmings and the gay familiar carols. I had to make a dozen phone calls to track down each person's Christmas gift name to determine whose name Philip had drawn. And, of course, the person that had his name was given another. "Strange," I say to Harry while I'm wrapping the presents, "that Philip was the one who organized the Christmas gift drawing this year." Harry shakes his head and keeps his eyes glued on the TV.

Cathy and Peggy, sensing my difficulty, overcome their own reluctance to celebrate and go with me to pick out the Christmas tree. Later they help hang the ornaments on it. Harry keeps resisting any attempt at holiday preparations. I force myself outside to hang lights and red bows around our front picture window. The decorating requires a tremendous amount of energy, but gradually everything gets done. We talk about baking Christmas cookies, but they never get made. It's the only thing we skipped.

Sue calls a few days before Christmas to ask if she could bring a memorial candle which she received as a gift after Philip died. "Can we have it burning during the party? It will represent Philip's presence in spirit?" I tell her I would like that. "Do you think it would be too sad if we said a prayer for Phil when we light it?"

"I don't think so. All of us are going to be thinking about him. It might be easier to have a special time set aside to talk about our feelings. I'd like to do that right at the beginning, before we open our gifts."

Mary and Mike planned to spend Christmas with Mike's parents, but changed their minds after Philip's death. Peter flies his family back again from

Boston. We all need to be together.

Christmas Day turns out to be part holiday festivity and part group therapy. As soon as the whole family is assembled and provided with a beverage and hors d'oeuvres, Sue announces we will have a short prayer time to remember Philip. "I feel Philip here with us in spirit." With quiet reverence she lights the tall vigil light which is decorated with a painting of Jesus. We place it on the drop leaf walnut table in a central position in the living room so it will be visible to everyone. Sue leads us in prayer.

When she has finished I read a short meditation which I found in a pamphlet at the Survivors of Suicide meeting. It's written in the form of a letter to a missing loved one. One of the passages I find most helpful is, " . . . Many of us feel that we are in some way responsible for what happened to you. You can be sure that if we were responsible for your life, you would be with us today . ."

For a few minutes a heavy silence smothers all speech and activity holding even the small children motionless. Tissues appear in trembling fingers to dab at watery eyes. Mary breaks the silence. "It's hard living so far away. We only saw Phil once or twice a year, so when I got back home after the funeral I kept forgetting he was dead. You know, it's not like he was around all the time so I would miss his not being there."

"It's the same with me." Peter's words are interrupted by his short sniffing noises. "After I moved to Boston I only saw Phil at Christmas and summer camping trips. Jim and I were talking about that when I got back home after the funeral. The fact that Phil won't be around anymore doesn't want to sink in."

"The fact that he's dead hit me hard when he didn't show up for hunting at the farm last month." Judie's soft, high pitched voice is quiet as she speaks. "It felt like there was a big empty hole where he was supposed to be."

Jardo, sitting next to Judie by the big front window, nods his head. "Hunting's never going to be the same."

"That's for sure," adds Chris in his resounding baritone. He has his arm around Karen who is crying softly into a tissue. Mike fixes his gaze on each speaker in silence. Unbeknown to us he is conceiving a visual image of 'the Hole' where Philip used to be.

"I guess it doesn't matter if you live far away or close. Even I keep forgetting he's dead." Sue is sitting on the couch between Josh and Sarah with a bewildered look on her face. "I keep expecting him to walk in the door, or sometimes, I'll remember something important I want to tell him, completely forgetting he's not here any more."

Peggy speaks quietly, her eyes staring dreamily at a scene only she can see. "I keep picturing him walking in the front door of our new house the day he picked up his tools. He had this wide impish grin on his face. He looked so happy that day. Sometimes I stop and stare at the door wanting him to walk through it again."

"You know what I wish?" Heads turn towards Cathy. "I wish we could go camping with Philip one more time. I want to help him gather kindling and have him teach me to split wood. All that stuff I used to take for granted. I never appreciated how good it was to be with him." Voices murmur in agreement.

Sitting together talking about Philip is bringing his presence back to us, filling a need, easing the yearning. I would have been content to do nothing else that day, but I see the children edging toward the presents under the tree trying to see which ones are tagged with their name. They've been patient and quiet long enough. I interrupt with, "It looks like the children are getting anxious to open their presents." I want the children to have a happy day.

In the flurry of passing around presents, the sounds of paper ripping and children squealing as the room fills with the wrappings and ribbons they are tossing about, we smile and even laugh. I hear exclamations of pleasure as each one peers into their surprise gift package and discovers who has drawn their Christmas gift name. For a while it's almost like old times.

With Christmas over we start girding ourselves for the last week of January, and Philip's thirty-fourth birthday. I've always had the family over for his birthday dinner. I'm not prepared to give it up so I invite everyone over for his party. "Isn't that kind of weird," asks Cathy, "giving a birthday party for someone who's dead?"

I considered this myself and have my answer ready. "Last week fifty thousand Milwaukeans showed up to celebrate Martin Luther King Jr.'s birthday. There's no reason why we can't celebrate Philip's birthday."

Cathy's doubtful expression breaks into a broad smile. "Then I take it you will serve buffet?" It takes a moment for the meaning of her joke to penetrate my gloom. Then we laugh like a couple of giddy school girls. God, it feels good to laugh again.

I make a dinner complete with birthday cake and candles. After we eat I light the candles and we all sing 'Happy Birthday' to Philip one more time. We watch the candles burn till they become small stubs in danger of burning the frosting. In a flight of insanity I'm hoping Philip's spirit will breathe from heaven to blow them out. Geri rescues the scene by saying, "Sarah, you had a birthday this month. Why don't you blow out the candles?"

As soon as our days' off coincide, Sally and I meet for lunch. Straight off she begins, "I'm so sorry about Philip. No one should have to go through this." She slides her ample hips into one side of the booth.

"Sally, I had no idea grieving was so hard. It's not only the pain of losing Philip, there's all this other stuff.....getting rid of all his belongings, worrying about Sue and his children, trying to comfort my own children. . .and the worst part is remembering things I should have done for Phil. I feel guilty about so many things."

"You're not alone, honey," she says shaking a few brown curls out of place. "When Megan committed suicide I went through all of the above. It's all part of normal grieving. Nobody can believe what a morass of miserable problems are involved until they go through it themselves."

"I used to counsel bereaved relatives in the hospice. I thought I knew all about grief, the feelings, the stages, how to handle them; all the stuff they tell us in books, but I didn't know a damned thing about real grieving."

"After Megan committed suicide I went through lots of books about grieving. Most of them helped, and technically they were right, but they didn't get to the core of it. They can't. You know what they say, 'Experience is the best teacher. Well in my book, it's also the worst damned teacher."

"That's for sure. So is there anything that helps? Anything I can do to get out rid of this grief mess faster? I keep wondering if there's something I should be doing that I'm not."

"As far as getting through it faster, there's no way I know of, and believe me I tried. It's over five years since Megan died and I've just about gotten through with the pain and struggle." Sally has begun attacking her Caesar Salad while I poke my fork at a Chicken Stir-fry.

I feel my heart sink. "I don't think I can stand going through this for five years. Already I'm drinking too much brandy. . . trying to numb the pain. In five years I'll be a blooming alcoholic."

"I went through a couple of months where all I

wanted to do was sleep. I did nothing but go to work and come home and lie in bed. Here's when I got some really conflicting advice. My doctor wanted me to take tranquilizers to give my nerves a break. But my therapist said 'No!'. She said it only delays the inevitable. And once you come off that stuff, you have to take up all your grief work right where you left off. She insisted that the only way to get through grieving is to 'Go through it till you get to the other side.' I'm glad I had enough sense to take her advice." Her voracious appetite shows me she has indeed gotten to the other side.

"My life will be a wreck before I get to the other side. I can't make decisions or concentrate on anything. And Harry.....he won't talk about it at all. He's become a grumpy old man. Cathy's getting an ulcer and Peggy has one bout of flu after another. Right now I don't see how we'll ever get through this."

"I know. There was a time when I felt like that. It's like being in a deep, dark hole and you can't see any way to get out. I was certain life could never be good again. You know, looking back now, grief seemed to block off everything but itself. I couldn't foresee anything but pain and misery for the rest of my life. I was convinced I would never be happy again. You can't believe me now," she says reaching across the table to hold my hand, "but your life will straighten out, and you are going to be happy again. You're doing the right things. Keep going to your grief group. Talk out, or write out all your bad feelings. And when good feelings pop up, write them out too."

Sally hails the waitress to order a slice of French Silk Pie. "I see you're not eating very well," she says eyeing the pile of food remaining on my plate.

"Food doesn't appeal to me any more. And it takes so much energy to eat. If I didn't have to cook for Harry, I know I wouldn't cook at all."

"I didn't eat much for a while either. Your appetite will come back. It all comes back... unfortunately", she adds patting her hips.

"Another thing that will help you; this is important... You've got to get out now and then and do something fun."

"I don't feel like having fun. I just want to sit on the couch, sip on brandy, and think about Philip."

"I know. But you've got to force yourself to do things at this point. Keep forcing yourself into fun, creative activities, and gradually your feelings will follow. I know, because my therapist kept goading me to get out and about. Little by little I started to feel alive again. Now, I'm actually happier than I was before. I can see that plowing through all this rubble has made me more perceptive to life's value, its opportunities, its. . . its potential for joy."

I shake my head wearily. "I can't imagine I'll ever be happy again."

Sally nods, her mouth turning up in a faint smile. "That's what I thought too. Believe me when I tell you, you are going to be happy again. And there is an end to grieving. Take it from someone who knows."

She scoops up spoons full of pie, and fills me in

on how well her husband and children are doing. "The kids are really taking off now that they're finished grieving." While I wait for a container to wrap up my stir-fry, she tells me about their graduate courses and job promotions.

Sally and I part with a long hug. "I'm going to be checking in on you often," she says before we part. Thank you God for giving me a friend like Sally.

❯❯ 10 ❮❮

Bleeding Hearts

Winter drags on with an ample provision of gloomy, gray days for mourning. The pain of loss is no longer constant. It washes over me in waves forcing me to cry a few minutes, a few hours, and occasionally an entire day. Some spells come without any apparent reason; others are brought on by objects and everyday happenings that have some way of connecting with Philip. I reach over to turn off my radio alarm clock one morning and burst into tears when I remember that Philip gave it to me for Christmas the year he drew my name in our gift exchange. Going to the basement to read the water meter I look down to see his name scrawled on the cement block wall in black crayon—one of his first writing accomplishments.

Every floor of our house contains reminders of Philip's life with us: the spice rack he made that I reach up to daily for a seasoning; the wooden message holder, an Industrial Ed. project, fastened to the wall next to the kitchen phone; the small cross he fashioned out of pink wax and stuck on the family room window. The hot sun of many summers has melted it firmly onto the glass.

I mention to Peggy one day that I keep seeing people who look like Philip. I see Philip driving by in his red Honda, Philip walking down an Eastside street with a load of books slung under one arm, or a glimpse of Philip among a crowd of shoppers in the mall. "Sometimes I think I'm obsessed."

"I know what you mean, Mom. I keep seeing him all over the university. I never realized before how many people there are who look like Philip."

Harry gets angry when I tell him about seeing Philip. "It doesn't do any good to keep going on about Philip," he tells me. I suppose he's right but I can't seem to get away from it. Philip's presence clings to me at work, at the movies, even in church. I can't sing hymns in church without bursting into tears. Sue confesses to having this same reaction. It puzzles us.

Sue starts complaining about a continual achy feeling in her lower back. "I think it's from driving so much. I spend a lot more time in my car now that I'm running all the errands Phil used to do. I bought a special support cushion for the back of my car seat. I hope it helps."

Sue is not the only one reporting new and unusual maladies. "I keep getting this sharp pain right here in the middle," Cathy says one day rubbing a central spot on her upper abdomen. Her teeth are clenched in a grimace of discomfort.

"That sounds like the start of an ulcer, Cathy.

You've been pretty stressed out over Philip's suicide, haven't you?"

"I just can't get it to make sense, Mom. There's no way this should have happened. That's not the way Phil was." She shakes her head vigorously.

I search my brain for a tidbit of the motherly wisdom that generally flows from my lips and end up saying helplessly, "I can't get myself back in gear either."

We stand facing each other silently for a moment. "I keep thinking I'd be okay if I could just work this out inside me," she says. "It's like one of those ancient Chinese riddles with some obscure solution. I can't come up with the right answer." She reaches up into the top shelf of the kitchen cupboard for my bottle of antacid.

"You ought to see a doctor, Cathy.

"I've got an appointment with the doctor next week to see if I'm getting an ulcer. Meanwhile I'm drinking lots of this stuff," she says holding up the bottle.

At my next 'Survivors of Suicide' meeting I talk about my depression and how it feels different from grieving. "My counselor says it's repressed anger at Philip," I tell the group. "But I'm not angry at Philip. How can I be angry? He was sick. He couldn't help what he did."

"You're absolutely right," agrees another member. "Our loved ones who take their own lives need our compassion...our understanding. They were suffering."

"Yeh, but you have to admit a lot of us have been angry at someone or something—sometimes other relatives, or ourselves, sometimes life in general."

"That's right. Anger's a part of grieving. We have to remember that before we start taking it out on someone."

"And we have to be tolerant if someone gets angry at us."

During this discussion our group leader has been paging through her resource folder. She holds up a newspaper clipping. "I found this article in the Times a couple of weeks ago, and I think it clarifies some of the excellent points you've all been bringing up." The group quiets down as she reads:

"When a popular California radio host and disk jockey took his own life recently, a newspaper columnist received severe criticism for her L. A. Times article, 'SUICIDE IS WRONG'. In it she cites the pain and confusion he inflicted on his wife and children, his parents and siblings, his co-workers, and countless faithful radio listeners who admired him.

"Her article states: 'Whether it was his intention or not, each individual family member, friend, acquaintance and fan received a notice of rejection that told them who they were and what they provided for him was not worth sticking around for.'

'And, wasn't everyone in the country who heard the news a bit shaken that a person who seemed to have it all, didn't want it? Don't we all get the message that what our nation and its communities have to offer isn't enough to make life worth living?'

'We can no longer ignore the profound trauma that is inflicted on our social community when one of our members deliberately drops out by taking his own life. The pendulum has swung too far in supporting an individual's right to choose life or death.'"

"Counter attacks poured in from the medical and psychiatric community testifying to the emotional and/or physical illness that drives someone to end his life. 'A person who takes his own life is so deeply immersed in his pain he can't think rationally...' and another...

'Modern research into the causes of suicide has generated a humane shift toward compassionate treatment of the suicide victim and his family. It is a much needed change from the chastising laws and attitudes of past centuries.' ...and still another comment, 'Suicidal behavior has taken its place among the ranks of psychological and/or physiological diseases that require understanding rather than condemnation.'"

"Which one of these attitudes is correct?" asks our group leader looking around the room. None of us volunteers an answer. "There's some truth in all of them," she continues, "and it's finding a delicate balance between these conflicts that makes our healing so difficult."

It's Easter Sunday before our family gets together again, this time at Sue's house. I haven't seen Judie since Christmas so the first thing we do is find a quiet corner of the house for some conversation. She tells me she's worried about Jardo.

"Where is Jardo?" I realize I haven't seen him since we arrived.

"He refused to come. He and Theresa had a fight just before we were going to leave and he said he'd rather stay home alone."

"Theresa? She's never been a troublemaker."

"Oh, it's not so much Theresa. It's him. He's been so darn moody and crabby lately he's hard to live with." I notice her face is becoming etched with worry lines. She looks older, and tired.

"It's Philip's suicide. He can't get over it." She sets her jaw firmly and inclines her head. "I was afraid this might happen. Jardo's the kind of person that can't let go of something till he has it thoroughly analyzed. And . . well . . none of us can understand this."

"I know. I think about it all the time myself, but Jardo . . sometimes he blames himself for not being more supportive of Phil . . . sometimes he gets mad at Sue for having that argument with him the night before he died. . . "

We stare silently at the expanse of countryside visible through Sue's den window thinking about

Philip...about Jardo. "And how are you doing, Mom?" she asks looking over at me.

"Not so good. Kind of tired and depressed. I've been wondering too, if there was something more I should have done for Phil. This whole business makes it hard for me to keep my thoughts focused. It's especially scary at work when I'm taking care of the sick babies and premie's. A mistake there would be disastrous."

She gives me an affirming nod. "My job at the factory is so routine it's hard to forget anything, but sometimes I wonder what I'm doing studying to be a chemical engineer. I'm acting so flaky I might blow something up." We smile, but the uneasy look doesn't leave her face.

"We're bound to get over this." I try hard to sound convincing. "Especially you and Jardo, you're so young."

"Yes," she says with a deep sigh. "I hope so."

Easter heralds the return of Spring and nature retrieves her colors. I lag behind in the dirty gray winter of depression even as I watch bright tulips, daffodils, and snow drops push up to brighten my yard. The Bleeding Heart bush Philip planted next to our house one year on Mother's Day turns full green and blooms, but the sight of the delicate pink puffs sends me into spasms of grief. I know I'm grieving because I will never see or talk to Philip again in this world, but I'm aware that there's something else wrong. A sickly turmoil is brewing inside me, but summer is in full bloom before Bill helps me analyze its chemistry.

I catch myself meditating on crummy things I did to Philip when he was a child. My memory replays every negative interaction between us, every angry or foolish reply I ever made to him. Now with the hindsight of raising seven more children and my nursing studies in psychology, I see with dreadful clarity the mistakes I made. I long for some miracle that would give me the chance to live my life over so I could do a better job of mothering Philip.

I no longer read grief books. Instead I search library stacks for books dealing with psychology and psychotherapy. I'm desperate to figure out what went wrong with Philip and what was wrong with me as his mother. As summer heats up I plod through mazes of self-searching accompanied by the words of psychotherapists whose book titles sound hopeful.

After one week-long session of merciless introspection I convince myself that I have failed miserably as his mother. I call Bill to tell him that I know I am to blame for Philip's alcoholism, his depression, for his final tragic mistake. "If I had been a better mother he never would have killed himself."

Without a moment's hesitation he replies, "That is the Jesus Syndrome." I forget the recitation of my failures with Philip and puzzle over his remark.

"What is that supposed to mean?"

"You are trying to take all the blame for Philip's death so he won't be responsible for it himself."

"You think that's what I'm doing...? Then you don't think I was a bad mother to him?"

"Absolutely not. You loved him and did what you thought was right for him at the time. That's all any parent can do. And, don't forget, you had eight other children and a husband who demanded your time and energy at the same time."

As he speaks fogs of misconception clear out of my mind making way for a more realistic focus on the situation. "Well . . . then I don't have to do this to myself. Since Jesus took on all the blame for our mistakes, He's already taken care of Philip."

"That's right." His words and the certainty of his convictions, sink in, take hold. Gradually my crushing burden of guilt lifts and I feel ready to get on with living.

Harry and I tend to our garden, he concentrating on his tomatoes and cukes, I on my flowers. We've had no rain since April and must sprinkle gallons of water on them daily to combat the eighty and ninety degree heat. I watch my roses bud, bloom, and wither in one day. My peonies last only three days, fried by the blazing sun. Seeing my flowers die makes me feel sad, thinking about Philip, thinking about death. Life is a great burden. My own consciousness at my center is the heaviest burden of all.

I no longer believe that I alone am to blame for Philip's death, but there are remnants of uneasiness clinging to my conscience. I talk to Bill about my feelings. "If I made such grievous mistakes in evaluating Philip's condition, I might be making other serious errors in judgment."

"I've been waiting to hear from you. I expected you'd be going through these difficulties. Besides normal grieving you're working through the problems that a suicide leaves in its wake. You continue to shoulder a certain amount of responsibility for Philip's death."

"I suppose you're right. I guess I'm still mad at myself for not realizing how sick he was. I never dreamed he would take his own life."

"You couldn't have known because Philip chose not to communicate his distress to you. And remember, I told you that you've buried your anger toward him and you're not able to let it out. That's going to keep bothering you."

"I think you're wrong about that. I'm not angry at him. How can I be angry? He was sick."

"These things take time." Like a prophetic oracle who has made his pronouncement, Bill declines to discuss this further. Now, instead of being angry at Philip I'm angry at Bill for being so damn certain about my inner workings when I cannot figure them out myself. I hold my anger inside while we exchange polite goodbye's.

By mid-summer I've read a shelf-full of psychology books without finding *the answer* that will heal my troubled psyche. An especially hot summer afternoon finds me browsing between the tall stacks of an air-conditioned bookstore. It's a comforting place. Hidden by the dull brown of the high bookcases, I'm soothed and quieted as I move slowly about on the soft dark carpeting. Today I feel attracted to the section marked 'Spirituality'.

Directing my gaze across the rows of titles, my eye comes to rest on "The Cloud of Unknowing". The title has a familiar sound to it, some phrase or passage I've heard before. Nothing specific registers in my memory but I feel drawn to the book. A quick perusal of its contents informs me that it's an ancient Christian writing on contemplation whose author is unknown, probably an obscure monastery abbot writing instructions for his novices in the twelfth century. "Far out stuff", I think, but I feel compelled to buy it.

During my next free hour at home I curl up on the corner of the couch with a cold orange soda and begin reading. From the first paragraph I'm intrigued by the calm simplicity of the thoughts laid out before me. They draw me into God's presence and hold me there as they counsel me in the way of abandonment to his healing love. I realize that these words are what I have been searching for. In the words of Alcoholics Anonymous the passages say to me, "Let go and let God." I begin to wonder if Philip's untimely death fits into some mysterious plan of His that I can't possibly understand at present.

When I sit with the open book in meditation I feel rested and secure and I have no questions. But once back in contact with my daily round of work and interactions with others I become an irritable mix of depression, anxiety, and indecision. My trust in the goodness of life, and in myself, was broken when Philip killed himself. Even with the consolations of God's presence, the wise counsel of Bill, Sally, and my support group, that broken trust is a long time in healing.

It rains during the last week of August breaking the long spell of hot, dry weather. "I thought I'd sleep better when the nights cooled down, but it doesn't seem to make any difference," I complain to Harry one morning after an especially restless night.

"I know what you mean," he says in a low grumpy voice. I've been hearing his bed springs creak during the night with his tossing about. His bedtime brandy hasn't been relaxing him the way it used to.

Sleepless days and nights are affecting my alertness at work. I write down my plan of care for my shift, highlighting it in bright colors so I won't forget anything. One night as I stand next to an Isolette in the nursery preparing a special formula for its occupant, a tiny growing premie, I feel myself tipping to one side. I grasp the Isolette rails to keep from falling over. When I feel steady I take a step to one side and the objects about me swirl dizzily.

"I need some help in here," I call out to the charge nurse in the next room. She stops what she is doing and comes hurriedly, probably thinking one of the babies is in trouble. "Something's wrong with me. I'm dizzy," I explain. She makes assignment changes to cover my babies and in five minutes I'm in a wheelchair on my way to Emergency room. The doctor discovers my blood pressure is a whopping 160/104.

He listens to my heart, has me sit up, checks my pulse. "Probably an inner ear infection." He prescribes a tranquilizing agent to calm the inner ear fluid and sends me home with orders to rest for a few days. The medication makes me feel drowsy and I sleep better. I return to work, taking the medication whenever an occasional dizzy spell recurs.

❧ 11 ❧

First Anniversary

September twenty-fifth approaches. Hard to believe it's been a full year since Philip's death. I'm surprised how fresh the pain feels. My mind trails about endlessly recalling details of his death. I become increasingly forgetful, wandering from room to room wondering what I was going to do. I drive to the store only to forget what I was planning to buy.

I notice changes in my children. Cathy has a severe ulcer attack and returns to the doctor. Peggy fights with her brother Mike when he eats her last muffin. They're barely speaking. Harry is even more grumpy and taciturn than usual.

Sue calls. "I've been thinking a lot about Philip. I don't want to be alone on the anniversary of his death. I arranged for a Memorial Mass in his honor at Holy Hill next Sunday. Do you think you could come out there to be with me, and maybe bring some of the family?"

We all join Sue at Holy Hill attending the Liturgy

with her, except for Peter and Mary who live too far away. I'm glad we are together. Like Sue, I need the support. We cry at church, we cry at the cemetery afterwards as we stare down at Philip's grave. We make no pretense of comforting each other. There is no way.

I open a letter from Peter dated September 30th:

"The anniversary of Phil's death has come and gone. It is still very sad when you stop and think about it. How was the Memorial Mass at Holy Hill? Wish I could have been there."

I answer Peter's letter the following week:

"The Memorial Liturgy was a pretty ordinary service. During the offering of the bread and wine the priest looked up and announced that the Mass was being said in honor of Philip. As soon as he said that Peggy burst into loud sobs. That started the rest of us crying, all except for Chris who stood by quietly with a strange look on his face. The people around us stared, not understanding what we were going through. No one can understand unless they have lived through it."
"After church we visited Phil's grave. I planted a pot of yellow Mums, so did Sue. Strange we should both pick out the same flower. The day started me thinking a lot about Phil again. I thought I was getting over it. How long does this go on?"

Impulsively, I reach up to my closet shelf for the grocery bag containing Philip's clothes. Carefully, I peel back the tape and look inside. I caress the soft flannel, run my hand over the coarse denim, reach down to the bottom and run my fingers along the edge of his shoe. "Philip, Philip," I whisper. "I want you here, wearing these clothes."

I come to my senses abruptly. Philip's been gone over a year. I should get rid of these old clothes. How many times did I counsel the bereaved family members of our deceased patients about disposing of their loved ones belongings? I hear myself saying: "Parting with your loved one's belongings is a major step in 'letting go'. If you haven't disposed of their possessions in about six months, it's best to get counseling to help you with that task."

Yeah, right! Determined to do the logical thing, I press the tape back into place and carry it toward the trash container. No! I can't let them go. "I'll save them, just a little longer," I think as I raise the bag up to my closet shelf once more.

At my next support group meeting I talk about being unable to let go of that one bag of my son's clothes. One man admitted he has left his wife's room just the way it was when she died two years ago. Some group members said they felt better getting rid of all the stuff they couldn't use right away.

Our group leader suggests, "When it comes to letting go of your loved one's possessions, it's probably better for each individual to go at their own pace. I find there's no hard and fast rule for this. For what it's worth," she continues, "for seventeen years I saved the belt my husband used to hang himself. It was just a few months ago that I looked at it one more time and thought, 'I don't need this anymore', and I threw it away."

After that meeting, I felt better about the bag of Philip's clothes on my closet shelf. I guess I'm not so crazy after all.

Another Halloween comes and goes followed by the church feast called 'All Souls Day', a day set aside to remember our dead loved ones. Kneeling in a gray fog of sorrow at Mass, I pray for healing and comfort. Instead, I'm suddenly charged with a hot flush of anger. "Damn it Philip! Why did you have to go and kill yourself? Look at how much pain you've caused everyone." I yell at him internally burying my face in my hands so no one around me will be disturbed by my appearance. "You have turned me into a sad person. You've made our lives very hard. And what about Sue? And Josh and Sarah who have no father? How could you do this to us?"

Immediately I feel his presence next to mine. I hear his voice just the way he used to speak, quiet and gentle. "Mom, I couldn't stand it anymore."

That's all. Just those few words, but the anger inside me drains away and a peaceful calming of my spirit takes its place. "Philip," I answer him in my heart, "I know how much you could stand. When you made up your mind to something your stubborn will saw it through to the end. I strain to imagine the terrible sufferings of your short life. If you say you couldn't stand it anymore, I believe you."

That night I dream that Philip is not dead, but is terminally ill with a few days to live. We are all helping to care for him. He's lying in bed propped up to a sitting position with pillows. I dress him in a new plaid shirt, comb his hair and take pictures of him. "I want to have these pictures to remember you by after you are gone," I tell him. Then, for the last time, I spill out all the words I have been longing to tell him since he died. Words I have written down in my journal, secrets whispered only in my heart.

I wake up peacefully, filled with a sense of relief, as if I have completed a task that has been nagging at me. It's the way I feel after I've finally gotten around to cleaning the basement, painting a room, or paying off the balance on my Mastercard. When I took care of terminally ill patients in the Hospice I used to talk to them about putting their house in order, tying up loose ends, saying their goodbye's. That's what I've been wanting to do with Philip. Now my house is in order and I can rest easy.

The first Sunday morning in November is dark with thick snow clouds hanging low in the sky. A cold gust of wind finds its way up the sleeve of my bathrobe as I hold the front door open looking for the early morning paper. With a deep breath I catch the frosty clean smell of snow in the air. No sign of the paper yet. Harry and I are up early to prepare for the double celebration we're having today. It's his sixty-fourth birthday and this coming week we'll reach our fortieth wedding anniversary.

I hear him in the kitchen making a pot of coffee. "How's your back this morning?" he asks as I walk in to scout up some breakfast. While bending over to mop up the bathroom floor yesterday I made a wrong move and felt something unpleasant happen in the lower right side of my back.

"It feels pretty sore yet." I attempt to pull myself erect but sharp stabs of pain shoot up to my right shoulder and down my right hip. "I still can't stand up straight."

"Oh, oh," Harry turns a worried face away from the coffee pot to look at me. "Are you going to be able to make the pasties today?" Cornish pasties made the way my grandmother taught me are one of his favorite dishes.

"No problem. The girls are coming early to help me and I already have the beef cut into cubes."

After breakfast I scuffle into the living room and sit on the couch with a heating pad wrapped around my lower back. While I wait for the warmth to draw out the stiffness, I go through my routine of morning prayers. Time alone with God refocuses me into the right channels before I begin my day. As usual my mind drifts off into thoughts of Philip. Gone over a year now but still hovering in the corners of my consciousness. Another party he will not attend. Everyone will miss him but no one will say anything. We are making an effort to put the joy back into our celebrations.

Halfway into the morning it starts to snow big

wet flakes. "This is too early for our first snow," says Harry as he stares out the kitchen window watching thick flakes come to rest on the dry leaves we haven't raked off the back lawn. "I hope Judie and Jardo will be able to drive in from Prairie Creek."

"I hope so too. Well, I'm sure they'll call soon if they decide not to come." I keep working on the eighteen pasties. Cathy and Peggy arrive in time to help me assemble the last few and we put the first batch into the oven. Soon the heavenly aroma of hot pastry crusts with their simmering contents of onions, beef, and potatoes fills the kitchen and wafts invisibly into the far corners of the house.

Chris and Karen arrive carrying bags of chips and a large platter of taco dip, which Chris has made himself. "It's one of his specialties and it's delicious", says Karen smacking her lips. Sue comes next with Josh and Sarah and bags of raw veggies to go with the pasties.

"Driving's not bad," announces Sue. "The snow's melting as soon as it hits the roads." Mike comes in soon after her carrying a large flat square package with a birthday card sized envelope taped in one corner.

Harry passes around drinks and we're all diving into Chris's taco platter when Judie and her family arrive. I'm relieved to see Jardo with them. "We ran into a few bad spots where it was coming down heavy," Jardo explains as I gather up their coats and jackets. After the first loud flurry of greetings we settle them down with drinks and munchies to enjoy a half-hour of visiting before dinner.

"Maybe Dad can start opening his presents now," says Cathy during a lull in the conversation.

"Yes!" Harry seconds the motion adding, "the pasties will be ready to eat soon." I send Mike and Chris into the spare bedroom to get Harry's surprise birthday present from its hiding place. They come back pulling the three foot by five foot gift wrapped box. "What in the world . . ." Harry wonders out loud as he tears off the wrappings and gets out his pocket knife to pry open the heavy cardboard. He looks surprised, but pleased as he pulls out a partially assembled exercise bike. "Thanks everybody. I haven't been getting enough exercise since Geri took her bike over to the other house. This is just what I need."

"We didn't bring your birthday present with us today, Dad," says Chris. "We're giving you our power lawn mower to replace that one you can never get started. We got ourselves a new self propelled one." He grins as he looks over at Karen.

She laughs, her blonde curls bobbing. "He says I'll be able to cut the grass by myself now."

"Anyway we didn't think you'd need a mower anymore this year. I'll bring it over next Spring."

"That's great." Harry laughs and points to the window. "Looks like what I need today is a snow blower." We all turn to the big front window to look at the large flakes still falling.

Mike approaches Harry with his flat square package. "Here you go, Pop. Happy Birthday."

"Ah, haa," Jardo says looking at the package.

"Could this be a Mike Olive original?" Murmurs of agreement follow as Harry unwraps the gift.

Harry's eyes mist over as he holds up the framed painting. "Thank you, Mike. This is very good." I hear the faint sucking noises of air being drawn quickly all around the room as Harry holds up the picture for all to see.

It is Michael's vision of 'The Hole' where Philip used to be. A rough hewn workbench spans the canvas with a light coming from above focusing the eye on the empty space in the center. Above, tacked akimbo on the wall, is a snapshot of Philip on his hands and knees building tinker toys with baby Josh. Slightly to the left of center Philip's hunting knife stands erect, its point buried in the surface of the bench. In the shadows his hunting clothes hang in readiness on the back wall.

A somber stillness permeates the room as the picture is passed around. "He left a big hole in our lives," Judie says softly as she passes the picture on to Chris.

"It's hard for me to think that he won't be coming up hunting this year," says Jardo. Deer season is only two weeks away. He looks over at Sue. "Will Frank be coming hunting this year?"

"He didn't know if he could make it. We'll see. But I'll be coming with Josh and Sarah." Sue has been learning how to handle a rifle and plans on joining the hunt.

"Matt and I will be there for sure," says Chris.

"How about you, Dad?" Judie directs her question across the room to Harry sitting in the rocking chair.

"I don't know. My feet have been bad." He's been hobbling with plantar's warts and lately a touch of gout. "It's getting too hard for me to tramp around in the brush."

"Oh, come on," coaxes Jardo. "We'll give you the stand on the back porch. You get to shoot anything we scare out of the woods onto the back forty."

"Well, maybe I could handle that." Harry lets out an unconvincing chuckle.

As usual our party day goes too fast. Judie and Jardo leave early on their precarious drive over snowy highways to Prairie Creek. One by one most of the others excuse themselves and tramp off to snow covered cars. "I want to have a couple more Cribbage games with Dad," Chris tells Karen who is relaxing on the couch in the family room.

Karen tells me about the couch and new TV they have ordered for their own Christmas present, and about the new picture window they're having installed. Chris looks up from his cards to say, "We want to spend some money on you this Christmas. How about having a new floor put in the kitchen and family room?"

Our vinyl floor is worn and pitted from thirty years of traffic. Looking around at it I have to admit it's a mess. "That would be great. I always thought a wood parquet pattern would look nice in this family room."

Mike turns off the TV and looks interested in our

conversation. "You know what would look great in the kitchen? A brick pattern, in either reds or browns."

"Why don't you think about getting the whole kitchen fixed up, maybe getting some new cabinets," suggests Chris.

"I could use a new countertop too." I start getting enthused about the project.

"I can take the baseboards off myself," says Chris, "and take them home to sand and stain."

By the time we finish discussing the kitchen remodeling it's after ten. We walk together to the living room to help them on with coats and say our goodbye's. About six feet before we get to the front door Chris turns, puts his arms around me and gives me a warm affectionate hug. I am a little surprised. I can't remember the last time he hugged me. It feels good. I look up at him, "Bye Mom," he says his eyes shining with love.

"Bye Chris." He turns and follows Mike and Karen out the front door. Harry and I watch them get into their cars and wave into the darkness till they're out of sight.

With the excitement of the party over I become increasingly aware of my sore back. "I'd better sleep with the heating pad on my back tonight," I say to Harry. "That should make it better by morning."

It doesn't. Harry drives me to the doctor who diagnoses a strained back muscle and orders me on strict bed rest for ten days. The pain meds and muscle relaxant make me drowsy, and my thoughts are fuzzy. For the rest of the week I put plans for the kitchen project aside, figuring I can't do anything about it flat on my back. My thoughts about Philip's death take on a hazy, peaceful resignation. "At last," I think, "I'm getting over my grief."

❧ 12 ❦

Premonition

By the following Sunday my back feels fine. I stretch out on the couch to read the morning paper. Bright sunlight streams through our South windows making gleaming square patterns on the hardwood floor. I barely settle into a comfortable position when the phone rings. I reach over my head to the end table behind me grab the receiver. "Hello."

"Hi, it's Chris. Have you gotten any estimates for the new flooring or cupboards yet?" I explain about being laid up with a bad back.

"Use the yellow pages," he says sounding irritated. "Let your fingers do the walking. You can have someone come to the house to show you samples and give you an estimate."

He sounds so anxious I feel guilty about procrastinating. "Okay," I promise. "I'll start looking in the phone book right away." We discuss plans for the family Christmas party. He and Karen want to hold it at their house this year. I warn him that it's a big commitment involving at least thirty people, but he refuses to back off. "Okay Chris, we'll talk about this some more, and I'll call you as soon as I get estimates on the flooring and cupboards."

I raise myself stiffly and head for the back hall shelf to get the yellow pages. My slippers swish softly as I slide my feet carefully across the floor to avoid jarring my back.

With the yellow pages spread open next to me on the couch, I copy down the names and phone numbers of three flooring dealers. Before completing the last one, I realize that something about this project doesn't feel right. I force myself to copy down a fourth dealer, which makes me more agitated. "I'm not ready for this," I think as I slide the phone book off onto the floor and go back to reading the paper. My uneasiness increases. I can't concentrate on reading. Maybe I need to move around a bit.

I carry the heavy book back to the hall shelf. Seeing Harry across the room I start to tell him how nervous the flooring idea makes me feel. Open mouthed, ready to speak, I change my mind. It will just disturb his reading and it doesn't make sense anyway. By now my back muscles are tightening so I scuffle to the bedroom, take a pain-killer and lie down.

The medication usually relaxes me quickly, but this time, my anxiety increases, tensing my stomach muscles and tightening my back. "What is so scary about remodeling the kitchen?" I ask myself in disgust. "Just pick out some materials and patterns and put up with a little mess." Rationalizing does no good. My agitation grows, making it hard to lie still.

I begin to feel afraid, as if something dreadful is about to happen. I pray for a while, ask God for the return of peace, but no relief comes. No matter what I do for the rest of the day I feel trembly inside, and scared. I've nearly given up brandy as a grief-aid, but at supper time I resort to drinking 'E&J' on the rocks. Still without relief. "All right, God," I pray at bedtime. "If you want me to feel nervous it's okay. Your will be done. Just, please, keep us all safe."

The next morning I feel perfectly rational. After breakfast I call flooring dealers to get the estimates Chris wants. The floor estimates range from $1,600 to $2,900, and the new countertop and refaced cabinets are over $3,000. "This will cost a lot more money than Chris imagined," I tell Harry, quoting him the estimates.

"I don't want the kids spending that much money on us."

"I don't either." This must have been what made me so nervous yesterday. Harry and I discuss what we could use in the kitchen that would be more reasonably priced. "I could use a new bread box," I say. Harry scrunches up his face to show me what a bad idea that is. "I know! You always cuss when you have to get down on your hands and knees to find a can of soup in the bottom cupboard. How about putting a cupboard with those new slide-out shelves in that empty space where the dishwasher used to be? You could pull out a shelf easily and pick out what you need."

"That sounds like a great idea. I'll bet Chris could build something like that himself."

I call Chris as soon as he returns from deer hunting and tell him about the costly estimates we received and about our decision to ask him to build the cupboard with sliding shelves instead. "Okay," he says, not sounding disappointed at all. "That's what we wanted, to get you and Dad something you'd really like. I'll start looking around at cupboards and get some ideas." We talk about some other plans he has made for Christmas day, then say goodbye.

With the coming of the Christmas season my spirits begin to lift in anticipation of good things to come. In a spurt of ambition I clean the kitchen and take measurements for the new cupboard Chris is going to build for us. With energy to spare I say to Harry, "How about doing some Christmas shopping this morning?"

We spend a couple of hours at the Mall picking out gifts then go to our favorite restaurant for a late lunch. By the end of the day we are tired, but in a happier mood than either of us have enjoyed since Philip's death. Before I go to bed I call Peggy to discuss some secret plans we are making for celebrating Cathy's birthday the following week.

It seems that I've just fallen into a deep, restful sleep when off at a distance a sound begins sending persistent fingers of noise into my brain. The sound comes closer, becomes louder, a vibrating middle C tone at persistent, annoying intervals. The vibrations begin registering in my mind as a bell ringing. As I return to full consciousness I realize the bell is our telephone. In the dark, quiet of the night it sounds raucous and annoying ... more urgent than usual.

I roll over on my side to look at the glowing red face of the digital clock on my dresser. Exactly 2:04 A.M. Irritation over the loss of my good night's sleep discharges a surge of adrenaline to fully awaken me. It must be the hospital calling me to cover some emergency at work.

Slipping out of bed quietly so as not to disturb Harry, I tiptoe into the living room and pick up the phone by the couch. I struggle to mask my irritation. "Hello", I say as pleasantly as possible at that hour of the morning. My voice is low and hoarse from sleep.

"Hello, this is Joanne. Chris has been in an accident.

"Who's Joanne?" I think, confused. This doesn't sound like anyone from the hospital. The voice repeats.

"This is Joanne, Karen's mother. Chris has been in an auto accident. He's in critical condition at the County Hospital."

"Chris? My Chris?" Her words refuse to make sense to me.

"Yes." Now I hear the shakiness in her voice. "Here's Karen," she says.

Karen's higher pitched voice comes on choking out words between sobs. "Chris has been in an auto accident. They say he's badly hurt."

"Oh God, no! Not Chris!" In the silence of the

darkened living room I feel my throat tighten, my stomach cramp down.

Karen keeps talking rapidly and crying. "I was so worried about him. It kept getting later and he didn't come home. I knew something was wrong. Then the hospital called …" her words break off; she's crying too hard to continue.

I hear Joanne's quavering voice again. "We're driving to the hospital to see him now. He's at County Memorial Hospital."

I choke out, "We'll meet you there." My words are breathless, strangled.

I remain sitting on the couch, a frightening sense of dread filling me, pushing down on my heart. I know it's time to move, to follow through with the actions required of me. With great effort I rise. My body feels immobile. I walk back to the bedroom, bracing myself with one hand against the wall, and sink back down onto my bed burying my face in my pillow. "Please God," I pray, "Please, no. I don't want to do this again. First Philip… now Chris?"

Suddenly my mind snaps back to the task at hand, to Christopher lying somewhere in a distant hospital. I have to keep going. Chris and Karen will need me now. I push myself up and turn on the small dresser light. Harry is still sleeping, his face turned toward the opposite wall. His respirations are wheezy and rasping from years of smoking.

I reach over to his shoulder and give it a gentle shake. It's his turn to hear the news, to feel the pain. I lean over him and push the day's new trauma into his left ear with the words, "Chris has been in an accident. He's in critical condition in County Memorial Hospital. We have to go there right away."

"Damn!" he explodes waking up with a start. He rolls over on his back opening his eyes a slit to look at me. "Damn," he repeats. "I don't need this."

His anger sends another shard into my already jagged emotions. My own anger rises. He's being selfish and stubborn. "Chris is hurt. He needs us. If you're not coming, I'm going by myself."

He sits up in bed and stares at me, his eyes bloodshot, watery, tired. My irritation softens. His sleep dulled brain begins to clear and I see comprehension steadying his gaze. "I'm coming," he says, his drooping shoulders heave a sigh of resignation.

We begin to pull on our clothes. He is sitting on the right side of the bed, I on the left, our backs to each other. Silent. He ties his last shoelace and stands up. I'm already stuffing things I think I might need into my purse. "Which County Hospital? he asks breaking the silence.

I'd forgotten to ask. I had assumed Milwaukee County, but it could be Waukesha or Kenosha.. Karen or Joanne could have told me. "I don't know," I say feeling annoyed with myself. I ponder this new problem a moment. I grab my purse and hurry back to the living room phone. I get information to give me the right phone numbers. I dial the first hospital number.

"My son, Christopher Olive, has been in an accident. I think he's in your hospital.

"I can check for you," she says competently. After a brief pause she says, "I don't see him listed here. I'll see if he's been transferred to an inpatient room." Seconds tick by. I fidget with the zipper on my purse. At last I hear her say, "Your son Christopher is still in our Emergency Department." Her voice is strangely distant, toneless, quiet.

"Is he very badly hurt?" I ask fearfully.

"Yes. He is."

The sinking feeling begins again, dragging my heart down with it. "Thank you," I murmur dutifully before hanging up the phone.

Except for discussing the route and the exit ramp numbers, Harry and I speak very little during our drive through the dark suburban streets. I'm afraid my thoughts would be too disturbing to him if spoken out loud. Perhaps he's feeling the same apprehension. But then, I'm not sure. He rarely says what he's feeling.

We swing out onto the expressway and cross the bridge above the dark expanse that is the Milwaukee River Valley, heading south toward downtown Milwaukee. The tall Victorian houses lining the freeway are dark except for an occasional porch light or a yellow-orange square outlining a second floor bedroom window. We pass three or four cars coming from downtown before reaching the Marquette Interchange. Glancing east down Wells Street and Grand Avenue I see bright security lights in the stores and colored neon signs atop them blinking frantically in vain. There is no one on the streets to see them.

Up ahead to our left I see the large square light that is the Allen Bradley clock, sometimes playfully referred to as the 'Polish Moon'. As we near it I see it's past two-thirty. Harry is barely going the speed limit. I feel impatient. "Can't you go any faster?" He makes a grumbling noise and stubbornly keeps his foot pressure steady on the gas pedal. Anxiety gnaws at me. I'm anxious to be with Chris. I begin to imagine what he will look like, what shape he'll be in—battered, bloody, ghastly pale, unconscious. I try to brace myself for the first look at him. We'll pull him through, I feel sure of that. But it will be another Christmas ruined for the family.

The last time I talked to Christopher was over the phone a week ago. "Mom," he said eagerly, "I'm excited about having the family Christmas party this year." I sounded a bit dubious about the idea, but pleased. It would be a big load off my shoulders. "And be sure to get me the measurements for the new cupboard so I can get it finished for Christmas." Christmas is now three weeks away.

We leave the city lights behind and drive through a dark stretch of countryside. As I stare at the straight empty highway unrolling before us, I begin to have a mysterious sense of Christopher's presence seeking mine. I feel him near; hear his voice saying my name. He needs me. "Chris, you're going to be okay. I love you; God loves you. You're safe." I hold him close, reassuring him. It's comforting. His presence fades. I'm alone.

Again I urge Harry to drive faster. Now I'm

certain we have to get to Christopher in a hurry. Somehow he's reaching out to us for help. "Chris needs us," I tell Harry.

After what seems like hours of driving, I begin to fear something has gone wrong. "Harry, we should have been there by now. Are you sure we didn't take a wrong turn?"

"I don't see how we could have. I've been watching the signs and I'm sure I turned off at the right exit." I strain my eyes trying to make out every street sign we pass. The houses are closer together now and I see lights and buildings ahead. We're driving slowly, looking for the hospital. To the left I see a brightly lit sign 'County Memorial Hospital'. We pull into the drive marked 'Emergency' and brake to a halt in a parking slot. Without waiting for Harry I jump from the car and head for the double doors marked 'Emergency' flagging down the first person I see. "We're looking for Christopher Olive. He was in an accident."

The woman I have accosted is wearing a dark flowered dress and appears to be a clerical worker. She calls to a white uniformed young girl down the hall. "They're looking for Christopher Olive." Harry has caught up to me. "He was admitted to Emergency during the night."

"I'll find out where he is," the nurse says pleasantly as she turns to walk back down the hallway, disappearing around a corner at the end. Several long minutes pass before she reappears accompanied by a youngish blonde man in a white coat, an orderly, or perhaps a Resident MD serving out his time in ER.

His face is solemn. Without changing his expression he says in a flat tone, "Come with me." He leads us through a maze of corridors, then down a long hallway to a closed door marked 'Waiting Lounge'. He opens the door to reveal a small square room with compact chairs and couches lined up against the walls. Sitting on them forming a semicircle around the back of the room are Karen, her mother and father, and her two younger brothers. They look toward us as we enter the room. The resident backs out and closes the door.

Before we can say hello Karen rises from her chair and runs to me throwing her arms about my shoulders. Crying in a loud voice she says, "He didn't make it! He didn't make it!" Harry is standing open mouthed in the center of the room. The faces of the others are a blur.

"No," I shout. "This can't be true."

"He wasn't even driving," Karen goes on, "it was a friend of his from work. His friend was drinking. It wasn't even Chris's car." We cling to each other, me stunned, she crying loudly.

"No!" I shout again. "I can't believe this." I back away from her, pulling out of her grasp. "I want to see him. Where is he?" I rush to the waiting room door and push it open shouting, "Where is my son?" I look up and down the corridors. I'm shouting at empty hallways and blank closed doors. Harry is standing beside me.

A white suited man slips noiselessly through a doorway down the hall to peer at us. "Who are you looking for?" he asks speaking softly.

"Christopher Olive," I answer, still shouting. "He was in a car accident. I want to see him." To myself I think angrily, "What's the matter with these people. Don't they know where he is? Don't they know he's here?"

"Come in here," he says leading us a few steps down the corridor to a closed door. He holds it open for us. Harry and I rush into the room then stop, all motion, all thought arrested, frozen in a timeless scene that engraves itself forever in our memories. There, in the center of the cold, white tiled room, lying on a high narrow stainless steel table, is our son, Christopher. Except for his strange pale yellow color he could have been sleeping. Lying on his back, eyes closed, lips slightly parted, his countenance in repose, he is covered up to his neck with a clean white sheet.

I approach the table. Timidly I reach out and touch his hair, brush it back from his forehead. He does not move. I touch his cheek. Cold and hard. My boy. Gently I pull the sheet down on the right side, just far enough to see the old scar from the surgery he had on his dislocated shoulder. It's my Chris, my darling boy. He is dead.

Then I see the large gauze bandage at the back of his head. It's soaked with blood. Drops of blood are oozing from the lower edge of the bandage forming a widening dark red pool on the shiny table. Christopher's blood. The blood that contains his life. Harry is looking at the blood, too. He stares at Christopher. He does not touch him.

"I'm sorry," says a male voice behind us. We turn around. The man in the white scrub suit is still there. I realize now he is the doctor. "We did everything we could to save him. He stopped breathing on the way to the hospital. We did open heart massage on him but could never bring back any signs of life." He is speaking intently, his brows knit in concentration. "He received a severe blow to the back of his head which caused a skull fracture and possibly a broken neck. There's not another mark on him." He is shaking his head 'no', looking distressed, as if there should have been more he could have done. He apologizes again, "I'm very sorry."

We stare at the doctor, then at each other. I see the tears, pain, confusion in Harry's eyes. I know they are in mine too. "Do you know how it happened?" Harry asks.

"The police officer told us there were witnesses that saw the car going about sixty miles an hour down a side street. The driver apparently tried to make a left turn, lost control, and slammed into a parked car. Your son in the passenger seat hit the back of his head on the door frame. It happened a little after 1:00 A.M.

I'm picturing the scene as he talks, hearing the screeching of brakes, and scraping metal, seeing Chris's head slam against the post between the front and rear doors on the passenger side. It's the killer seating position in a car. I remember learning that when I started driving. My mind becomes lucid, detached... "And the driver? Was he hurt?" I ask.

"He was dazed. Minor shock, a few bruises, but otherwise unhurt. His eyes were glazed—looked like he might have been under the influence of drugs or alcohol, but that could have been from shock. After we finished checking him over the police took him away to the station to file charges. They were convinced he was drunk. They said charges would most likely be 'Homicide by Intoxicated and Reckless Use of a Motor Vehicle'. They'll get a blood alcohol level of course."

In spite of my pain I feel my heart stir and move out in a brief surge of pity toward this unfortunate young man. "It could have been Chris driving," I think, and a scene from another accident ten years earlier flashes through my mind.

It's New Year's Eve, just nine days after Christopher's eighteenth birthday, a significant milestone in the days when eighteen was the legal drinking age. Chris had borrowed my Pontiac to drive to his job grinding hamburger at a wholesale meat packing plant in Glendale. At 5:30 P.M. the Glendale police call to tell me Chris was in an accident and is being charged with 'Driving While Intoxicated'. "That can't be," I protest. "He was just supposed to drive my car to work and back."

When I arrive at the station Chris is still undergoing questioning. He's crying and shaking but he's not hurt. I stand nervously by the officer's desk while Chris repeats his story.

His co-workers insisted on giving him a drink (he swore it was just one) to celebrate the New Year. After the drink he offered to drive a friend home. It wasn't much out of his way. A light snow had begun to fall. They were halfway there when Chris felt my car sliding on the slippery film of snow, heading straight toward a fire hydrant. Turning the wheel to correct the slide he skidded to the opposite side of the street, bounced off an elm tree on the parkway and continued sliding up the front lawn of a red brick bungalow, not stopping till the car crashed into the house.

Mike goes with me the next morning to see the car. There's no doubt about it. It's totaled. Mike stands next to it shaking his head. "I don't see how those two could have walked away from this one."

The accident changed Chris. He was required to attend weeks of punitive driving classes in lieu of having his license suspended. He became a cautious driver. Began to look at life more seriously. Started making plans for his future.

His future? ... Plans?... The new TV and couch he and Karen were getting, the cupboard he was making for Harry and me, the big Christmas dinner. . . all so trivial now. . . But there were big plans: remodeling his own home at age twenty-eight, pursuing a brilliant career as a computer systems analyst; and children, they wanted to have children. . . ALL GONE. . . . What a fragile piece of imagination is our future. . . .Now I see with dreadful clarity the transient nature of our lives.

I'm back in the cold white room looking down at the ending of Christopher's life. The doctor has stopped speaking and turns to leave the room. "I'm very sorry," he says once more before he leaves us alone to grieve.

We stare numbly at each other, then at Chris. I walk slowly around the table gazing at his lifeless form. I touch his shoulders, his head, brush my palm over his hair, bend over and rest my cheek against his cold forehead. "My darling Christopher," I whisper to him. "you were a good boy. I love you so much." I strain to fill all my senses with his presence this one last time. Tears are streaming down my face. It's hard to breathe. Too soon it's time to go away and leave him there. Harry takes my arm and leads me back to Karen and her family.

Back in the waiting room I embrace Karen. "It's all right if you want to see him," I tell her. "I mean he looks okay. Just a bandage at the back of his head."

"No!" she cries backing away, a look of horror darkening her blue eyes. No! I don't want to see him dead." I notice she is wearing his watch. It dangles loosely about her thin wrist.

"Did he have the last rites?" I direct the question to Carl, Karen's father, and to Joanne. I feel they will understand my concern. I have spent years hauling the children to church, teaching them to pray, and worrying about the state of their souls.

"We had them page the hospital chaplain," says Carl, "but when he got here and found out that Chris was already dead he became angry. 'This is the Sacrament of the Sick', he told us. 'I can't give it to a person who is already dead.' I asked if he could just say some prayers over him but he wouldn't do that either."

Frown lines deepen between Joanne's brows as she adds, "Even if he wasn't supposed to give 'Last Rites', would it have hurt him to say a few prayers over Christopher?"

"At the very least he could have given the rest of you some words of consolation. I mean, that's part of his job too."

"He was so rude I was sorry we had called for him. He made us all feel worse," says Carl.

"That's very bad," I agree. I rage and weep inside at this unexpected cruelty.

Everyone is standing now, putting on their coats. As they get ready to leave, Carl offers Harry his hand shaking his head sadly. Then, as if trying to make some sense of it all, he says, "I guess Philip wanted a Cribbage partner." Harry nods his head, attempts a smile.

⟫ 13 ⟪

Support Group

We agree to get in touch at 10:00 A.M. to discuss funeral plans. We go back to our homes dreading what lies ahead. Now we must share this tragedy with family and friends. It's nearly five o'clock Saturday morning when Harry and I get back to Milwaukee. Our first stop is our Eastside house, where we begin the painful task of waking our remaining children to tell them they have lost another brother. As the shock and pain strikes the heart of each one, our own pain is compounded.

"No, Mom not Chris," says Mike when I wake him from a sound sleep. Mike and Chris have become very close during the past couple of years, more so than when they were growing up in the same house together. Philip, Pete, and Mike were the oldest boys. Chris was the little brother who kept getting in their way. Mike whispers half to me, half to himself, "I only have one brother left."

Next we awaken Christopher's younger sisters, Geri and Cathy. Peggy is not home. "Not again," protests Cathy. "Not Chris. This isn't fair." When Geri hears the news her hazel eyes fill with tears and she turns her face into her pillow sobbing.

When they come downstairs we group around their small kitchen table and decide what to do next. They help me find the phone number of Janet's parents in Illinois where Peggy is spending the weekend. Janet is Peggy's best friend and longtime roommate. They planned to spend the weekend in Chicago getting an early start on Christmas shopping. I decide the kindest thing to do is tell Peggy the truth about Chris. She would be angry with me if I didn't.

Her voice is a quiet monotone when she is able to answer me. "I'll come right home, Mom."

As I did last year when Philip died, I make long distance calls to tell the other children they must come home quickly. Cathy, Geri, and Mike look for the phone numbers while I mentally piece together phrases that will break the news gently. I find myself starting out by saying: "Chris has been in a car accident." To my mind it seems to soften the blow that is to come. Before they can say anything I tell them the whole truth, "He is dead." After the crying out, the denial, I explain the few details of the accident that I'm aware of.

Our oldest daughter, Judie, speaks to me in a voice she keeps quiet and controlled. After consulting with Jardo, she informs me they can't drive from Prairie Creek until Sunday. Jardo must complete his shift at the Post Office today and they must make arrangements for someone to tend their farm animals. Peter, Jill, Eddie and Molly, will fly in from Boston this very afternoon. Mary in Duluth screams when I tell her the news. Just a year and a half older than Chris, they were very close growing up together. I knew this would be hard for her. She starts the long drive with Mike and seven year old Carli soon after I call.

Grief is still fresh with Philip's wife, Sue, but I know I must call and tell her. She'll want to know. "You'll have a gang there," she says thoughtfully. "I'll make a pot of chili and bring it over for supper." She'll come in the afternoon with Josh and Sarah.

By eight o'clock we're back at home. I don't eat, sleep, or notice when dawn eases away the darkness of this night. I no longer feel pain. I'm tense and jittery; my nerves go 'Zzinngg' at each encounter with noise or effort. Cathy, Geri, and Mike have come over and are making coffee and munching on toast. Their red, puffy eyes remind me that I haven't cried since I left Christopher lying in the emergency room. I feel too exhausted to cry. I never realized before how much energy crying requires.

Harry slumps in his favorite chair in front of the TV in the family room. With his handkerchief held up to his face, he is seemingly engrossed in the early morning news and weather. I retreat into the living room and sink into a corner of the couch. I feel eerily detached as I lean back against the cushions. The children seem to move about me as if they are actors on a stage. "Not children," the thought strikes me. "These are young women, and Mike, a mature man.

Cathy brings her coffee into the living room and sits down on a chair in front of the big window facing the street. She gazes out at the bare snowless tree lined street, then turns and looks about the room. "I can't believe this is happening to us again," she repeats several times at short intervals to no one in particular.

I know I ought to say something to Cathy; push some words together to comfort her. The ones that come to mind seem contrived, phony. She would see past them. "No," I murmur. "I can't believe this is happening to us either."

"Why Chris?" asks Mike who has walked in and placed a plate of toast and a cup of coffee on the small drop leaf table across the room. He seems to direct the question to me. "Phil had problems. That was bad enough. But why Chris?"

"My intense young man," I think looking across the room at him and wondering how to reply. Mike has always dived into problems head on, unable to rest until he has worked out a solution that satisfies him.

"Why Chris?" I repeat after him, pondering this new question. I analyze it as a detached spectator. Coolly removed from the tragedy, I can see why Christopher died. "Chris loved adventure," I tell Mike flatly. "He began taking risks as a toddler. He was never afraid, never thought about getting hurt, much less dying. You know how he used to disappear for hours on secret adventures, how he would sneak down into the basement and make bottle rockets."

"Yeh, and he did some pretty dangerous things with his motorcycles when he was in high school," Mike agrees.

I give him an answering nod. "When you think about it, he could have been killed a hundred times over."

"You're right," Mike answers slowly. I see his fist unclench and come to rest next to his plate of toast; his jaw relaxes. I watch understanding flow in to calm his grief filled eyes. Christopher's eyes were just like Mike's. I stare at Mike. It's almost like looking at Chris... same dark brown wavy hair, the long straight nose with a hint of the Mediterranean protrusion across the bridge. I can still hear one of Christopher's wedding guests teasing Karen about getting them mixed up.

In a flash of remembrance Mike says, "Just last October we went biking together. Chris was behind me riding in the middle of the street. When I turned around I saw a truck barreling down behind him. I yelled and made motions at him. Then he turned and saw it. Pulled over just in time. He could have been killed then."

"Yes," I nod. "I used to think he had this sense that life was a fun adventure, kind of like a game. That he could do whatever he wanted but he wouldn't really get hurt."

"I know what you mean," Mike says. "Like he was invulnerable."

"I used to think that was a great way to be,"

answers Cathy. She has pulled out of her reverie to concentrate on our conversation. "He had so much fun. He never worried about things the way I did."

Geri sits down next to me on the couch to listen. She tucks a pillow behind her and leans back, her right hand encircling a coffee mug. "I used to envy Chris," she says with a half smile that brightens her sad eyes. "He always seemed to be having so much fun." Her smile fades as she gazes thoughtfully into her coffee mug. "I used to worry about things, too." The room becomes quiet. I gaze into Geri's coffee cup and think about Chris and the way he was.

"There was a serious side to him too." Mike's loud voice startles me and I look up at him in surprise. He must think we are dismissing Chris too lightly. "When he wanted something he went all out for it. Worked his ass off till the job was done. You know, his hi-tech computer job, and buying their house last year."

"Yes," I say. "He accomplished very much . . ." I'm going to add "in his short life" but the words stick in my throat. Geri and Cathy join Mike in recalling Christopher's accomplishments. I retreat into myself. Somewhere in my subconscious I'm aware that what I told Mike about Chris dying is not the whole answer. "Dear God," I pray, "you protected Chris all of his life, why not today? What is different about today?"

"Mom. Mom." Geri's voice pulls me back from my reflections. I look over at her. "Mom, you need to eat something. How about some herbal tea and maybe some toast with jelly?" Geri is a nurse like me. We worry about other people's well being. Her features and light coloring favor my German ancestry. Philip and Judie inherited my blue eyes. Maybe Geri inherited my care giving tendencies.

"Okay, that sounds good," I say more to please her than from really wanting it.

"Is Red Zinger okay?"

"That's fine." I manage a smile. It feels good to be taken care of.

The phone rings. It's not yet nine o'clock. I pick up the receiver and hear Karen's voice. She hasn't slept either, or eaten. She says she's been thinking about the funeral. "I want Chris to be buried out near Holy Hill next to Philip. I think he would like that." Her voice cracks a bit on the last sentence.

"That's what I was thinking too. I'd like them to be together. We could have the Funeral Mass out at Holy Hill church before that. If it's okay with you I'll call and make arrangements." I feel satisfied that all is falling into place smoothly.

I call Sue to get the phone number of the pastor. "Father Gerard is gone and I don't know the new pastor very well but I can give you the phone number of his office."

"The pastor is not in the office today," the Secretary says curtly. Being Saturday I'm not surprised. "Can I take a message?" When I tell her that my son has died unexpectedly and we would like him buried at St. Francis Cemetery next to his brother she asks, "Are you parish members?"

"Well, no. But my son was and his wife still is."

"I'm sorry, that cemetery is restricted to parish

members only," she answers in a cold business-like tone.

"But his brother was just buried there a year ago. We want them to be together." I feel sure they will allow it under the circumstances.

Her voice is softer when she replies. "The pastor is out of town for a few days and I don't have the authority to allow this. Hmmm. . . , I'll give you the phone number of our parish council member who handles things like this. Maybe he can help you."

I dial his number immediately and repeat my request. I am stunned by his flat rejection. They have new rules he tells me. Members only. The cemetery is too small to admit outsiders. No exceptions.

A new pain crushes in on me. Phil and Chris can't be together. In desperation I call Sue and tell her what happened. "Can you help us? Maybe you could talk to someone you know out there."

"Since Father Gerard left they've got all new people on the council. I really don't know anyone I could ask. They've got all these new rules. I've kind of lost touch. I'm sorry, I don't know how I can help."

With sinking heart I tell the others. I feel like my church has failed us again—for the second time during this tragedy. "Now what?" I ask hopelessly.

"What about that place where we buried Grandma a couple of years ago? What was the name of that cemetery?" Geri asks.

"Holy Cross," I say picturing its wide expanse of well trimmed grass and shade trees. "Yes," I nod. "Grandpa is there too, and my sister and

Grandmother. Maybe we could get a plot near them. Then Chris wouldn't be alone." I look around the room at the others. No one looks enthused, but no one objects. I go out to the family room to ask Harry.

"Sure," he says with a shrug. "Why not? It doesn't really matter. They're all dead anyway."

"I'd better find out what Karen thinks."

"That's terrible," Karen cries when I tell her Chris can't be buried at St. Francis Cemetery. "But they're brothers; I can't believe they won't let them be together." It's a new sorrow for her heart too. I tell her about Holy Cross near my family members. She says she can't think of anything better.

"Do you want to have the Funeral Mass at that church where you and Chris were married?" My mind is churning now with unsolved problems.

"Well, not really. We don't know a lot of people there. Most of Chris's friends live around you."

"We could have it at the church down the street. Chris used to go there."

"That's fine."

"There's a good funeral parlor a couple of blocks from the church. I think I'll let them handle the arrangements." She agrees and jots down the name and address I give her. I hang up the phone and look questioningly at the children. No one seems to care.

Karen, her parents, and I meet at the funeral parlor at eleven o'clock. The funeral director greets us with the attentive cordiality I've come to expect from people in his profession. While not handsome, his face is pleasant; his blue eyes shine with warmth. He makes us feel taken care of. I remember feeling this way arranging Philip's funeral. I marvel at a funeral director's ability to convey a personal aura of compassion and still conduct business with professional efficiency. It must be emotionally draining—very similar to nursing.

"I'm so sorry," he says. "This is the hardest," he adds, "having a young person die." He's the most sympathetic outsider I've encountered thus far in our tragedy; or perhaps it was the doctor who apologized so profusely for failing to save Christopher's life..

The funeral director assists Karen and I in making the rapid decisions necessary to conduct the funeral and burial. It's just nine short hours since Christopher died. I know that we are engaged in making arrangements for his funeral, but it feels unreal. We are all here in some weird dream looking and speaking, acting and choosing.

Karen's parents are sitting on straight chairs near the director's gleaming walnut desk. Karen and I are sitting on a comfortable upholstered couch off to one side. The director hands us what looks like a thick photograph album. Instead of photos it contains 'holy cards', the little two by four ones with a serene picture on one side and a verse with the name of the deceased on the back. None of them seems suitable for Chris. Although I always considered him a morally upright person he was not what you would think of as religious or saintly. After paging back and forth Karen finally settles on a picture of St. Francis with birds and animals. "He liked being outdoors," she explains. I muse silently on how Chris used to hunt birds and animals with both gun, and bow and arrow, but I don't say anything. I don't imagine anyone will notice the discrepancy.

Next the funeral director leads Karen and I downstairs to a large display room filled with materials used at funerals. Carl and Joanne prefer to wait upstairs in the office. We walk softly through the room speaking in hushed tones. A faint sweet smell permeates the air, a cross between flowers and room freshener.

We pick out a polished hardwood casket. Somehow we both know that Chris would like it. "He always enjoyed making things out of wood," says Karen. . . .

"He would be proud of the workmanship on this one," I say.

We choose a medium priced vault in which the casket will rest. The director leads us back up to his office and discusses times and particulars for the services. He lifts burdens off our shoulders as he calls Holy Cross Cemetery and the pastor of the church, finding out available dates and times.

"It will be necessary for one of you to go to the cemetery to choose a plot and sign the papers," he says looking up at Karen and me apologetically. Karen flashes me a beseeching look.

"I don't want to do that. Will you?"

Seeing her need, a few molecules of strength surge through me, enough to carry out the task.

"Yes," I say reassuringly.

When the director has everything organized he looks around at us sadly. "I wish I could do one more thing for you. I would like to bring him back to you. That's the one thing I can't do."

As we have previously arranged we drive the few blocks to see Memere. We didn't want to tell her over the phone so she doesn't yet know that Christopher is dead. She was especially fond of Chris, and since Pepere died he and Karen regularly helped her with yard work, and the seasonal storm/screen and other tasks her house required. She invited them over for dinner often and loved to make them their favorite dish, chicken and rice.

At first she looks happy to see us all walking in her front door. Within seconds I see her smile collapse and her brows rise in questioning alarm. "What's happened? It's Harry," she cries. "Something's happened to Harry." Then she looks more closely at Karen and Joanne crying, and sees Carl there too. She went through this a year ago with Philip, and picks up her cues quickly. "Oh my God! It's Chris. Oh, no, not my Chris. He's not dead. Don't tell me he's dead."

We manage to convey to her that she has guessed correctly. When she is seated we explain how it happened. We sit with her for a while as she cries and moans, her petite five-foot frame shaking with sobs. Before we leave we promise to let her know about the Funeral Mass.

⫸ 14 ⫷

Once and Again

It's early afternoon when I arrive home. Peggy has returned from her Chicago jaunt and is now at our house with the others. I feel her thin shoulders tremble as we embrace. "I can't believe this is happening Mom."

"I know, I know," I say soothingly. "I can't believe it either. This shouldn't be happening to us again." Peggy was the baby of the family, the one I spoiled and fussed over more than the rest. It's been hard for me to 'let go'. I have to keep mentally reinforcing the fact that she is now on her way to getting her Master's Degree in Social Welfare. I lead her out into the kitchen to fix her some lunch.

Mike is stretched out on the family room couch sleeping, or making an attempt at it. I can't tell which. Harry is in his lounge chair next to Mike. The TV is off. His eyes are closed, his head lolling against the high padded back rest. Feeling unsteady and slightly nauseous, I go to my bedroom. Seeing my pillow lumped into a heap I remember sinking onto it with a desperate prayer just twelve hours ago. It seems far in the past now . . . a different lifetime ago. I force myself to lie still for an hour relaxing my tense muscles, but sleep won't come. My heart beats erratically. My nerves send frantic messages at the slightest thought impulse. Reaching under my pillow I fish out my crystal rosary and offer prayers for Christopher's safe entry into heaven, for Karen, and for all of us mourners. My fingers travel along the beads but my mind flits wantonly about the events past and conjectures those to come. I'm unaware that I'm grasping my crystal beads for the last time.

The front door bangs open and the chatter of young voices fills the house. Peter and Jill have arrived with six year old Eddie and three year old Molly. I hurry to the living room to greet them and see Peter's husky frame filling the front hallway as he gathers up coats and jackets. I wave a 'hello' to the children who are already vying for the attention of their young aunts. Jill and I embrace warmly and she says quietly into my ear, "This is terribly sad."

"Yes, I'm still having trouble believing it."

Peter greets me with open arms. I let myself relax in his bear hug. "Peter," I think, "how well we have named you, *the rock*." Sturdily built, assertive, competent, and self assured, he will cope well with this tragedy and help the rest of us get through it.

Peter put himself through Engineering School by age twenty-three, moved to Boston and got a high paying job as an electrical engineer, then went on to get his Master's. In between he came back home to marry, Jill, his pretty, dark-haired childhood friend and/or sweetheart since eighth grade. We always supposed he inherited his fair complexion and tightly curled brown hair from the Norwegian strain on Harry's side—taking after a couple of Harry's uncles. He looks like no one else in the family. Most of the children resemble the French relatives on Harry's side.

After helping Jill settle the children down with a box of toys hauled up from storage in the basement, Peter sits on the couch questioning us about the events that led to Christopher's death. "Who is this guy that did it? Have they got him locked up?" He is irate. Such horror done to his little brother. Not satisfied with our answers he calls the Police Department obtaining the exact location and description of the accident. He jots down notes as he talks.

"This guy works in the Court House," he says looking at his notes after hanging up the phone, "same place that Chris was working on that computer project. The story he tells is that he and Chris went out for dinner and a few drinks after work last night. They met some friends at a local bar where he had a couple of beers, then left to meet them again at a different hangout across town. He admitted he was going kind of fast to get there ahead of the others. They'd reached the 3200 block of 60th Street when he tried to make a left turn, lost control, and swerved into a parked van. Caught the van on the passenger side where Chris was sitting. They were in this guy's car, a brand new Accord. Totaled the thing."

"Did they get a blood alcohol level?" Mike asks.

"Sure did. It was 0.14 and the legal limit is 0.10, so they've got him on that. There were a couple of witnesses also who testified that the car was going about sixty miles an hour. The police figure they'll prosecute on reckless driving and speeding as well."

"That guy's done for," says Mike in a voice that resembles a cheer. "So is he locked up?"

"They're holding him in the county jail till the judge sets bail."

I watch Peter in silent admiration, awed by his efficiency at getting answers to questions that never occurred to the rest of us. I perceive that his anger and his determination to get to the bottom of this are his most effective coping methods for dealing with his grief.

We did a lot of charting in 'Nurses Notes' about our patients' coping mechanisms. If we're fortunate we learn coping skills by watching how our parents handle their problems; and we keep honing our skills as we grow older and our problems get bigger. The strength of our coping skill also depends on the state of our physical and emotional health when a crisis hits. Right now our family's coping mechanisms are close to bottoming out.

Peter looks up from his page of notes. "The coroner will be holding Chris's body till they get an autopsy done. Seems to be the law in cases like this. That'll set the funeral services back a day."

Mike and Peter continue discussing the legal implications of the accident, the possibility of bringing suit against the taverns for serving an already intoxicated driver. Peter gets out the phone book to look up the name of a lawyer friend of his in Milwaukee. Jill and I go out to the kitchen to prepare some snacks for the children.

The front doorbell rings again. Sue comes in with Josh, now thirteen, and Sarah eleven. Josh is carrying the enormous kettle of the chili Sue promised to make. I direct him to the kitchen, saying "hello" but not trying to hug or kiss him. He has the typical young boy's macho affliction of detesting outward displays of affection.

Sue greets me with a hug. "This must be hard on you, having another boy die so soon," she says in her usual frank manner. I appreciate her bluntness. It lets me talk about how I really feel.

"It's terrible. I'm not dealing with it well at all. I feel shaky and sick; things are falling apart. The only way I can manage is by keeping my feelings stifled while I get through the next few days."

"That doesn't sound healthy."

"It's not, but right now, the best I can do. It's good of you to come and bring us food. I know this is hard on you, and the children too, just getting over Philip. You don't need anymore grief and woe either."

"No . . . but I thought maybe I could be of some help to Karen, having just gone through this myself. And talking to her might help me work through some stuff too."

"She's staying at her folk's house. Her Mom says she hasn't been back inside her own house since Chris died. Her Dad's picking up Chris's good suit for the funeral and I said I'd come and get it around ten o'clock tomorrow morning. Why don't you come with me? It'd give you a chance to talk to her."

"Maybe I'll do that. I could drop the kids off here to play with their cousins."

"They'd like that. And I'd like your company."

Sue makes her way around the living room stopping to greet the others while I pick my way across the floor through kids and toys on my way to the kitchen. Eddie, with Josh now helping him, has fourteen model horses, each ten inches high, prancing across the polished oak floor in a race only he can see. Geri saved her allowances for two years to buy those horses during her period of horse love in grade school days. The big horses returned to their hey-day when the grandchildren began coming over to play. Eddie laughs with delight as Josh brings the synthetic horses to life and has them jump over furniture hurdles.

On one end of the room Molly, Cathy, Peggy, and Sarah are making up fairy tale princess games with two-inch wooden 'Wee People' and their wooden house and schoolroom, remnant toys from Cathy and Peggy's past. We have a room with shelves in the basement called a 'fruit cellar' stacked with these old toys. When the grandchildren started coming I was thankful I hadn't thrown them out.

Molly's little girl voice giggles and squeals, as

she makes her princess doll move about the imaginary castle Sarah has prepared. They make Cathy and Peggy laugh . . and forget.

I learned a long time ago that children perceive death in less complex ways than their grown-ups. When I was five years old my sister was killed in an accident on the way home from school. A truck driver swerved around a corner and didn't see her shining blonde curls in the crossing. Just seven years old, she was killed instantly. I sat on my front steps with neighbors while my mother and grandmother rushed to the scene a block and a half away. "Your sister has gone to heaven to play with the angels," a kindly neighbor told me. I remember thinking this was a wonderful thing to do, and having tagged along after her since I could walk, I wanted to go with her. A little later one of them asked me, "Aren't you going to cry? Your sister is dead." Still smiling I shook my head 'no'. Why would I want to cry on such an exciting occasion?

The children have been told that their Uncle Chris died in an accident, but the words carry no pain or terror to their hearts. In their world of 'now' they feel secure and happy. The young ones are puzzled that he can never come back from this far away place. I imagine they'll miss his presence at our family parties and vacations, at least for a couple of years. But there won't be the longing loneliness in it that we grownups have.

For Josh and Sarah, this death will not effect changes in their lives. Philip's death last year left them without the protective presence of their

Daddy. Sue has been taking them to a children's grief support group for help with their fears and unresolved questions.

Peter grabs the phone when it rings again. His voice becomes softer. From his words I deduce it is Karen on the line. "Ma," he calls after a few minutes, "it's Karen. She wants to talk to you."

"Do you have a rosary we can put in Chris's hands? I want him to be holding a rosary and we don't have a decent one." I think immediately of my crystal beads, the ones over which I poured hundreds of prayers for Chris and all the children. That is the one Chris must hold. It will be part of me going with him. I ask Karen how she'd feel about Chris holding crystal beads. She says that sounds okay. Later in the day I scrub the Rosary with soap and water, repulsed by the idea of bacteria and mold growing on it in the casket. Sometimes my nurses training gets the better of me.

Sue is motioning to me while I speak. She wants to talk to Karen. I hand her the phone and continue making my way to the kitchen. A glance at the wall clock by the back door tells me it's nearing four. I've got to get to the cemetery to pick out a plot before they close. I'm relieved that Peter volunteers to go with me. Every task I undertake now looms bigger than life size.

Peter and I reenter the house before six o'clock to the warm tomato spice smell of chili simmering on the stove. The delicious odor whips my digestive system into a feeling of hunger, the first I've had since Christopher died. Bowls of chili are already being passed around and I see fresh baked rolls, Jell-O molds, a pasta salad, and cakes spread about on the kitchen table. Seeing my surprised look, Harry fills me in. "Nancy and Em sent food over. So did some of your friends from church." Aside from warm embraces, kind words and prayers, I decide food is the best thing to give to the bereaved. People in mourning don't feel like cooking. Flowers are a close second.

The din of children playing and many voices chatting is replaced by the clinking of forks and spoons on plates and bowls. A little food in my stomach feels good. I'm relaxing a bit. Spacing out. Thinking.

Before the last bowl and spoon are set in the sink for washing, the doorbell rings. The door flies open as Mary, Mike and Carli enter. "Hi everybody! We finally made it." Their faces show the fatigue of their eight-hour journey. Mike's eyes are red and shadowed underneath from staring at the road, and perhaps crying. Seven year old Carli has a slight frown and doesn't smile when I kiss her. "Oh, Mom," says Mary when I come up close to greet her, "this is so bad. I don't want Chris to be dead too." She cries softly as she clings to me.

"I know. It's all wrong. This shouldn't be happening." I still have to bend over a bit to hold her. She's only five feet tall, and still looks like a little girl. Her ashen blonde hair falls in waves to her shoulders, framing her soft pretty features. Her usually smiling eyes are puffy and filled with pain. I hold her in my arms a long time wanting desperately to take away the hurt.

I turn next to Mike. "Thanks for coming so fast. We need you here." Mike is blue eyed, bearded, and comfortably handsome.

"Oh, sure," he says with his shy smile, "I wouldn't not come. This is hard on Mary, she needs to be with her family." He grew up with eight brothers and sisters, the same number of siblings Mary had. He sniffs at the invisible molecules of chili wafting in from the kettle on the stove. "Mmmm, somethin' smells good." Mike draws out his vowels a bit in the manner peculiar to rural Minnesotans.

"Sue brought a pot of chili. You're just in time for supper." They are waylaid all across the room by greetings and kisses. Geri follows me out to the kitchen to serve.

"You look tired, Mom. Sit down," says Geri. "I'll take care of them." I've avoided looking in the mirror. Geri's words are a clue to what I must look like. I see Carli, who's never hungry, reacquainting herself with cousins she hasn't seen since summer camping at Lake Wissota. Scattered across the country, I marvel at how fast the eight cousins pick up their thread of friendship when they meet every six months or so.

Between bites, Mary and Mike ask questions about Christopher's accident. Peter and Mike fill them in on the details. The facts engrave themselves deeper in my memory with each retelling. I allow myself a few tears.

We retire to the living room with cups of coffee

or tea. Herbal tea seems to sit better on my stomach than coffee. Molly has curled up on the cushiony green chair in the corner and fallen asleep. I look around the room at the faces of my children, at their spouses too. Lines of weariness and sorrow tracing over their foreheads and around their eyes and mouths make them look older. Eyes are red and swollen from crying. A few tears come as we group together for support, but mostly we just talk quietly, about Chris, about summer camping, about the old days when we were happy.

Suddenly Harry interrupts the quiet mood. "We've got to quit meeting like this," he says making a stab at lifting the gloom. A few smiles flicker across faces, but as fleeting as butterflies they are gone.

"You're right, Dad," nods Peter. It's too hard to smile, too hard to cry. We have cried so much there are no tears left. Our children appear to be drained and immensely sad. Now and then I see one of them staring with unseeing eyes, grieving quietly inside. We've known this house since each child's infancy. The air, once thick with happy memories, is turning heavy with grief.

A feeling of detachment begins enveloping me. We are here sharing the same thoughts, sorrows, words, but none of it feels real. We are all gathered together taking part in the same nightmare. One by one the dreamers excuse themselves from the scene and drift away to bed.

⋙ 15 ⋘

Read All About It

"Here it is," says Harry, spreading Sunday's paper out on the kitchen table. His finger stops midway down one of the obituary columns. Traces of lemony winter sunshine filter through the window and slant across the table highlighting the words:

'Olive, Christopher J.

Born to Eternal Life Dec. 3, 1988, age 28 yrs. Formerly of Whitefish Bay, Beloved husband of Karen. Beloved son of . . '

"This is it, " I say quietly to Harry. "This makes it real." I remember the shock of seeing Philip's name in print. Reading the obituary makes it final.... Cements all the facts in place so you can't pretend anymore. I relive the shock of seeing Philip's name last year. That was also a Sunday morning. The sun shining down on the columns was a brighter yellow, not as slanted, being an early Fall day. I knew how sharp the pain would be seeing Christopher's name this way, but I had to look anyway.

"Chris is the youngest one here today," Harry says running his eyes over the rest of the columns. "You notice they never actually say someone dies. They're all born to something." He edges away from the pain of it with his witticism.

I run my eyes over the dates and times of the funeral services and wake. "At least they have everything printed correctly." I feel a cramping pain in my chest with the next breath. I concentrate on taking deep breaths, and distract myself with putting cereal boxes, bowls, and sweet rolls out for breakfast. Harry folds the paper so the obituaries are on the outside front. He lays it down on the end of the table.

The phone rings. It's Sue. "I thought I'd better let you know that Judie and Jardo are driving straight to my house today. They decided to come here and spend the night. It's a shorter drive for them, and you already have a mob at your house."

The phone rings repeatedly after that as friends and neighbors wake up to read their Sunday morning paper. I never used to read the obituaries. I'm surprised how many people do read them habitually. We take turns answering the calls. The others get teary eyed explaining what happened to Chris. I put myself into a state of steely control. I shake a little but I don't cry.

We spend the rest of the day as quietly as we can with the phone and doorbell ringing. We receive more gifts of food and several floral arrangements. In spite of the small annoyance of answering the ringing bells we appreciate all the callers. It helps to know that many people loved Christopher and wish to comfort all of us who are grieving his loss.

Family members come and go on a variety of errands. Mary and Carli go to the nearby shopping mall. They need outfits to wear to the wake. Last year Geri, Cathy, and Peggy sought my advice on the proper attire for funerals. This year they know what to wear. Mike goes to get his car washed so it won't look so grimy in the funeral procession.

By six o'clock, all are drawn back to the big table in our family room, some for food, and some for emotional support. Gathered around the table we resemble a lineup of neurology patients recovering from simultaneous blows to the head. Some talk a little, some stare into space. But being together feels good.

Cathy and Peggy are the first to leave the table. Later I find them rummaging through the front closet. They pull out the large white canister filled with old photographs. I keep much of my memorabilia in this can by the front door so if the house catches fire I can grab it quickly and rescue it from the flames.

When the rest of us discover what they're doing, we join them in searching for Christopher's life in pictures. Peter, Mike, and I look through the bookcases for old photograph albums. Through the years I've managed to mount a few of the best snaps.

For some reason this pastime revitalizes us. We become obsessed with finding every picture taken of

Chris from the time he was born. Whenever one of us finds an especially great snap we hold it up to show the others, talking excitedly about what was going on in the scene. "This is Chris blowing out the candles on his green cake," says Cathy. "I made him that cake with the green frosting the day he got his 'green belt' in Karate."

"Here he is with his crew cut," says Mike shaking his head. "Those were the lean years when you couldn't afford to get us real haircuts. Remember, Dad, how you used to line us guys up Saturday mornings and practically shave our heads with your electric hair clipper kit?"

"There was nothing wrong with those haircuts," Harry says defensively.

"God, yes," Peter moans. "We all looked like little Nazi's."

"Did you ever notice Chris has this crooked little grin in all his pictures?" asks Peggy. "And his eyebrows are always raised a little as if something has surprised him." She passes several pictures around for our inspection.

"Ha!" says Geri. "Look at that devilish twinkle in his eye. He was probably planning something that would surprise us." We laugh while Cathy and Peggy agree wholeheartedly with that observation. Chris was merciless in tormenting his little sisters.

"Here he is doing his Al Jolson act," I hold up a picture of Chris who is down on one knee, his right hand over his heart, the other extended. "He was in about seventh grade when he started this. He'd suddenly plop himself in front of me and yell

'Mammy'."

"I remember that," Mary says gleefully. "We were doing 'Dixie' songs in the Spring Concert at school."

"Chris loved to sing," I add in case anyone has forgotten. He was in the choir all through grade and high school. His voice wasn't especially melodious, but it was plenty loud.

We laugh at Chris's funny antics, the spasms shaking trapped emotions out of our bodies. I find a manila envelope in the desk to hold the best pictures, planning to take them for showing at the wake and funeral luncheon. It's after midnight when I tuck the last picture into the envelope and go off to bed. I sleep restfully for a few hours, before disturbing feelings begin oozing into me like some unwelcome alien creature. Total consciousness returns, and with it comes the pain of loss.

⫸ 16 ⫷

Dream Sequence

We arrange to meet at our house and leave for the wake together. Judie and her family arrive around noon. This is the first time we've seen Judie and her family since they got to town. "How are you doing, Mom?" she asks. She holds on to me for a long time. There are no tears in her light blue eyes but I can tell by the red around the edges that she's been crying.

"I'm hanging on, and you?"

"'bout the same," she says with a slight nod.

I walk a few steps to greet Jardo. He gives me a limp hug. "Are you doing okay?" I ask.

"I guess," he says raising his shoulders uncertainly. His eyes look sad, his face a mask of restrained grief.

"This is hard on Jardo," Judie offers on his behalf. He lost another one of his hunting buddies." During their annual hunting forays, they had formed a close bond of friendship. Jardo hasn't recovered from Philip's death. But then, none of us has.

Peter comes over without Jill, Eddie, or Molly. "Jill thought it would be too sad for the kids at the wake. You know, seeing Chris like that and everybody crying, so she's keeping them home." I'm not surprised. She told me earlier that wakes of this type are never held in her Jewish tradition. She thinks they are a strange and difficult ritual to go through.

"When one of our relatives dies," she told me, "only one family member sees the deceased person and stays with the body until it's taken to the funeral home. You see, we believe it takes several hours for our spirit to leave our bodies, so we musn't be left alone during that time. Then, we hold a graveside service where all the relatives and friends attend. In the strict Orthodox Tradition the immediate family stays inside their home to grieve for seven days. They call it "Sitting Shiv-ah". The rest of the community supports them by visiting and bringing food."

Karen and her family are already at the funeral parlor when we arrive. They are all clustered toward the front near Chris, and all but one or two are crying. Karen is sitting in the center of an upholstered couch placed directly in front of the coffin, with her mother and father on either side of her.

I'm anxious to see Christopher. With a nod of greeting to the others I ease my way through till I'm directly in front of the casket. "My God, he looks handsome," is my first reaction. His flesh looks pink and warm, his head tilted up at a thirty degree angle on a white satin cushion, his slightly waved hair parted in the middle exactly as he wore it the last few years. His mustache is trimmed to symmetrical perfection. The corners of his mouth are turned up in the hint of a smile as though at any moment he will sit up, laugh, and tell us he was only pretending. I remember how he used to do that when he was playing with the grandchildren. He would lie on the floor pretending sleep while they tickled him, trying to make him laugh. For a moment my mind takes refuge in the fantasy that . . . perhaps . .

I get a sudden urge to hold on to him, to experience the warm embrace he gave me the last time we were together. I reach with my right arm to caress his face, my hand cupping around his cheek and forehead. The cold firmness of his flesh sends a chill up my arm. I pull my hand away quickly. His face feels greasy, not like real skin. Rubbing my fingers together I remember where I've felt this texture before. Craypas, the waxy chalk sticks my children used in their art projects. Craypas left in the refrigerator overnight to make them firm. Pulsing sobs begin shaking my body, I feel tears running down my face. Christopher is gone. Whatever form this is lying here, it is not my son.

The violence of my crying makes it hard to breathe. I feel weak and trembling. I stiffen my body, push the feelings back down inside and hold them firm. Frozen grief, locked away in my deep freeze of stifled emotions. I concentrate on breathing normally till I am able to move. My eyes travel down to Christopher's hands to see my crystal rosary gracefully entwined through his sturdy fingers. He holds the silver crucifix between thumb and forefinger. "It looks okay," I think, "not out of place in his masculine hands."

It takes a few minutes before I see the masses of red roses arranged in a spray across the bottom half of the casket, the part that covers his legs and feet like a carved wooden quilt. There must be thirty or forty long stemmed roses draped over it. They are adorned with a red silk banner with words printed in gold saying 'For My Dear Husband'. I become aware of the sweet scent of roses surrounding me. I look up to see another stand of red roses with the gold letters spelling 'For Our Dear Son', and yet another massive spray standing near the head of the casket with the words 'For Our Dear Brother'. I remember having told Karen to make arrangements for the flowers. She has poured out her love in roses, sparing no expense. The effect is startling, intense, beautiful.

I turn away slowly, my eyes sweeping over the masses of floral arrangements spaced around the walls of the room, filling the somber place with a profusion of color. Spectacular offerings of love and grief given as farewell gifts to our child. I see that more guests have been filing in while my back was turned. Feeling the tug of obligation to welcome them, I assume the roll of funeral parlor hostess.

I go to Karen first. She's still crying and now seems to be trembling uncontrollably. The flesh of her face has been sculpted away by grief making hollows under her cheekbones and a cavernous darkness about her eyes. I'm surprised to see that she's not wearing dark clothes but instead has on a bright green printed dress. Maybe I'm old fashioned thinking black is best. Young people do things differently now. I stumble over some words with which to console her. "Chris . . he looks so fine . . so handsome."

"I don't want him to be dead," she says in words broken by her trembling." Christopher's silver watch still dangles around her left wrist. It looks so large on her I fear that it will fall off if she lowers her arm. I see she's wearing a gold chain around her neck that holds Christopher's wedding band.

"I know," I say helplessly. What I know is that there are no words that will comfort her. "I don't want him to be dead either." I glance at Joanne, then at Carl. Their faces are contorted with pain as they look at me, then return their gaze to Karen. I imagine their distress is as much over Karen's grief as it is at losing Christopher.

"This is so hard on Karen, says Joanne. "She hardly slept last night and still won't eat anything. She's always been so thin she can't afford to lose any weight. Right now she's sticking close to Carl. She's always been her Daddy's girl." She shakes her head sadly. "It's a terrible thing to see your child suffer and not be able to stop the pain." We exchange knowing looks.

"That's the hardest," I reply. "Makes me long for the good old days when a bandaid and a kiss made everything okay."

Joanne agrees with me and adds, "Christopher

does look very fine."

Harry walks with me along the front rows of folding chairs shaking hands with Karen's brothers and sisters. We never became more than acquaintances with them, not close enough for more than handshakes. Karen's oldest brother and one of her brothers-in-law are crying continually. These must be the two Chris talked about so much. The ones he went boating and fishing with. It's obvious how much they cared for him.

I see our children walking along the aisles in small groups, going up to the casket to view Chris. They're wiping tears from their faces when they turn my way. As Carli returns to the back of the room with her Prairie Creek cousins I overhear her saying, "I don't like looking at dead people. They put too much makeup on their faces."

"Yeh, it makes them look like painted statues", says one cousin.

"That doesn't seem like Uncle Chris lying there at all," says another.

Harry and I spot his old high school friend, Jim, entering from the hallway. We used to party with his old school friends and their wives when we were first married. Haven't seen much of them lately. We heard Jim had lost one of his two sons in a car accident years ago. I'm surprised to see him here. "I had to come and see how you two are doing," he says. "I know how we felt losing one son, I can't imagine losing two."

"I don't know," says Harry shaking his head. "We never thought this would happen again."

The children's friends are arriving in droves, not only Christopher's friends, but the friends of our other children as well. I recognize most of the faces, but can't put names with all of them. Their eyes widen as they stare at the shocking sight of one of their peers lying dead. One of Geri's high school friends is standing open mouthed shaking her head. "He's really dead," I hear her mutter.

Families from my church community are here. "Bless them," I think, "they are so faithful about coming to these funerals." We exchange warm embraces.

"Let us know if we can do anything to help you," they say. I promise I will, not having the foggiest idea of what that might be.

I begin saying 'hello' to people I have never seen before. One of them turns out to be Christopher's boss. "You've lost a good one here," he says looking at me sadly. "Your son was the most capable systems analyst I've ever had." He shakes my hand as he speaks. His voice and bearing have the easy assurance of one who knows how to deal with people. "I've never put anyone so young in charge of setting up a massive computer system like this Court House project. Christopher did so well I knew I'd made the right decision."

"Thank you for telling me this. Christopher never told us much about his work. I'm glad he was doing so well." My heart fills with a mixture of pride and despair as I turn toward another grouping of people.

As I push myself from one group of mourners to the next, I have the sensation of having done all of this many times before. I feel the familiar cushioning of the soft parlor carpeting beneath my feet, hear the humming of voices hushed in sympathetic murmurs, see the boxes of tissue spaced at convenient intervals on tables about the room. Even the fresh flower fragrance that penetrates my nostrils with each breath strikes me as a memory from some other time and place. I feel myself to be an actor in a tragic scene I know well. When I approach grieving visitors I already know what I am going to say and what they will reply. I hold my emotions taut, not daring to feel what I'm expressing; not daring to admit into my heart the comfort others are imparting. "If I cry one more time," I think, "my insides will crumble and I will die."

Philip's best friend, Frank, comes close and I signal him with a desperate glance. He hugs me tight. Seemingly reading my mind he says, "Here we are again."

My control breaks and I let tears escape from my eyes. "What's happening to us, Frank? Is this some sort of curse?"

"I don't know," he says, his face showing the despair and confusion that I feel.

Suddenly my friend, Bill, is standing at my left side. "How are you doing?" he asks, his brow creased with worry lines. Relief and gratitude flow through me at the sight of him. How good he is to come and share my grief again.

"I don't think I can stand grieving any longer. I feel like I'm physically deteriorating inside." As I'm saying this my son, Mike, approaches on my right side and throws his arms around me sobbing.

"Help me, Mom. I can't take any more of this."

There must have been a last drop of courage in the wasteland that was my heart for I manage to say, "I'm here for you, Mike." Bill puts his arms around both of us and we embrace as we give and receive comfort and strength.

Literally hundreds of people pass through the scenes as the two days of services progress. Friends we haven't seen for years and neighbors who have moved away come back into our lives to offer sympathy and look at Christopher one last time. We meet many of Christopher's friends and co-workers we've never known before. They tell us of his expertise in setting up their new computer system at the Court House. Harry and I can't help feeling proud of him in spite of our anguish. The feelings of all who knew him are well summed up in the homily Peter gives at the Funeral Mass:

"My name is Peter. I'm Christopher's brother. I want to thank all of you for being here today. Your presence is a source of strength for Karen, my Mom and Dad, our families, and to Chris's closest friends; Mike, Randy, Michael, Matt, Bearclaw, and Damon.

I have many memories of Christopher - some happy, some painful, all precious. From my childhood I remember one summer afternoon when Chris burned his hand on a hot steam iron. I still remember the screams and how my mother held and rocked this crying child for hours in the living room.

"I remember one summer when we went camping and Chris, probably seven, got into some poison ivy and it swelled his eyes shut so he looked like a creature. My Dad drove him back to Milwaukee to see a doctor.

"I keep hearing stories about Chris. One time, as a small boy, he was throwing a ball around the living room and he broke the big front window. He tried to convince my mother that a woman with a baby carriage passing in front of the house had thrown a rock through the window. This was about the time he became "Quee".

"A more recent story is one you guys will be able to appreciate. At his birthday party a few years back, Chris blew out all of the candles on his cake through his nose. Well, no one ate any cake after that - only my Mom had a piece, but what are Moms for?

"I have recent memories of Chris, too; of camping at Lake Wissota this summer, fishing with him and Karen in their new boat.

"Chris lived life to the fullest. You could tell by all the things he had going on: fishing, hunting, Karate, woodworking, tinkering with old cars, dirt biking with Michael, his photography, football and baseball games.

"I was very proud of Chris's professional

accomplishments, as I'm sure you were too; of this massive computer project for the Court House in which Chris played a key role. After one of Chris's co-workers described how valuable and smart Chris was, I wished him luck on the project. He said, 'With Chris gone, we'll need more than luck'.

"As a brother, Chris was a source of silent strength to me. He was someone that I knew would always be there if ever I needed him. After we lost Philip last year, I felt better returning to Boston knowing that Chris would be here as a pillar for the rest of my family.

"Chris is with Phil now, and he's looking down at us right now. I'm sure that Chris would be very embarrassed over the big fuss that we're making over him.

"Life is fragile. Life is precious.

"Thank you Christopher for letting us share some special moments with you. Goodbye Chris, and thank you for the memories."

⁂ **17** ⁂

A Funeral Birthday

In a cruel twist of timing the day of Christopher's funeral and burial coincides with Cathy's birthday. A corner of my mind starts mulling over this conflict when I read the date set for the funeral, Tuesday, December 6th. I thought about the plans we'd made to celebrate her day, the presents already bought and wrapped, the cards attached to them carrying joyful and silly greetings. Damned ludicrous to bury one child yet celebrate the birth of another on the same day.

"What do you think we should do about Cathy's birthday?" I seek out the advice of Peggy and Geri after herding them into a private corner of the family room.

"Maybe something simple," Peggy says. "I know she's not feeling up to a party."

"We have to do something," Geri adds. "I wouldn't feel right letting her birthday go by unnoticed."

"Why don't you casually bring up the subject

with her, see what she thinks," Peggy advises. "You know, kind of feel her out."

Inwardly I cringe at the prospect of forcing myself through the trappings of a birthday party, but neither can I bear the uneasiness of disappointing Cathy. By Monday morning I know I have to take action. Her birthday is the following day. I approach her in the kitchen where she is stacking the breakfast dishes in the dishwasher. "Cathy, I've been thinking about your birthday party," I begin cautiously feeling like a swimmer sticking a toe in the water.

"I can't have a birthday party. We're all miserable about what's happened. Why don't we just forget it this year." Her expression registers amazement that I'm even considering it. I'm not overly surprised by her reaction. For two days I've been watching her wrestle with the pain of our new tragedy, watching it close off the easy openness of her outgoing personality. I push on with my words, knowing they must be said and somehow resolved.

"I don't feel like having a party either, but the trouble is people have already bought you presents and cards, and, well, they want to know what's going to be happening." I'm actually the one who wants to know what's going to be happening.

Cathy's brows knit slightly considering this. Her usual relaxed expression clamps shut and I see her jaw muscles working. "They can just give them to me whenever they feel like it. It wouldn't be right making people come to a party when they're grieving Chris."

Cathy has been an empathetic person since she

first became aware that there were people around her. Being that sort of a person myself, I know that her concern for others sometimes makes her ignore her own needs. This sets my motherly protective instincts in motion. I map out one of my tentative plans.

"Tuesday evening, when we get back from the funeral luncheon, I can serve cake and coffee and set aside a little time for you to open your gifts."

"I don't know," she says bending over to stack saucers in the lower basket of the dishwasher. She gives me a fretful glance as she straightens up. "It just seems wrong to make people do something happy on the day Chris is buried."

"What do you think Chris would want us to do?" I ask with sudden inspiration.

An uncontrollable smile loosens her troubled features. "Chris would be really disappointed if we didn't have a party."

It's late in the afternoon when we return home from the buffet dinner held after the burial rites. To join in her birthday celebration, Cathy has invited two girl friends she has been close to for many years. Two of Christopher's closest friends return home with the family also. I set the huge store bought cake in the center of the family room table and everyone assembles around it. There isn't enough room for everyone to sit down so some of the guests are standing behind a row of chairs. It takes two of us to light all the candles, but when they are all burning someone hits the light switch and all is dark except for the glowing cake.

As we break into a round of 'Happy Birthday' in varying disharmonious keys, our moodiness lifts and I begin to see sparks of joy reflected in the eyes focused on Cathy and her cake. By the time we get to the end of the song Cathy's broad smile shines over the candles as she is deciding on her secret wish. Flashes punctuate the darkness. Once again, we capture the moment in pictures.

Cathy successfully blows out all her candles with one breath. "All right." "Way to go Cath'!" We all clap. Her small nieces and nephews laugh and cheer.

After slices of chocolate cake are passed around and consumed we retire to the living room with coffee mugs in hand to watch Cathy open her presents. She exclaims with delight at each gift we have chosen for her. We respond with appropriate 'ooo's' and 'aahhh's' as she holds them up for viewing. While birthday cards are passed around for all to examine, I circulate with the coffee pot checking on who needs a warm up. I'm relieved that Cathy's birthday has come off with this much merriment.

Jardo rises from the chair in the corner of the room from which he has been silently observing Cathy. He walks over to her. His lean bearded face looks drained of emotion. As he passes in front of me the heaviness of his depression wafts insensibly into my consciousness fogging it like a breath of ether. Without attempting a smile he says, "Congratulations and all that good stuff. I hate to rush off like this but I have to be at work at the Post Office at five tomorrow morning." I help Judie find their three girls' jackets, mittens, and hats.

"I think we'd better be going, too," says Sue. "It's been a long day and these kids have to be up early for school. Give me a call if I can do anything to help," she says as I see her to the door. I promise I will.

Therese and Jennifer say goodbye to Cathy. I'm glad to hear them making plans for next weekend. Their company will be good for Cathy.

Damon and Chris, alias Bearclaw, are settled in their chairs absorbed in serious conversation with our Mike. They've been friends since grade school days, but it's been months since I've seen them. When Chris got married and left town four years ago they stopped coming around. Now they hang out with Mike over at the Eastside house or at Damon's.

Bearclaw looks at Cathy when she returns from saying goodbye to her friends. "Boy, I haven't seen you for years. What have you been up to lately?"

"All kinds of things. Peggy and I had a great trip to Portugal this Summer. We met Peter and Jill on the French Riviera and they let us share their hotel room for the weekend."

"Pretty wild," says Bearclaw with a low whistle. "What were you two doing on the French Riviera?" he asks turning to Peter and Jill.

"My company sent me to an international convention in France. I had to give a presentation on our implantable insulin pumps. We managed to squeeze Jill in for the price of the plane ticket."

"I'm impressed," says Damon. So what do you jet-setters have planned for next year?"

"The fun's over for me," says Cathy. "I enrolled in the Respiratory Therapy program at MATC. By the time I get my books and tuition paid there won't be enough money left to get me to South Milwaukee."

"Won't be much excitement for me either," says Peggy. "I'm back at UWM working on my Master's this year."

Bearclaw speaks up in a voice unusually quiet for him. "My life's never going to be as exciting again without Ollie around." Chris' close friends called him 'Ollie'—a nickname I haven't heard in years.

"He sure had a way of livening things up," agrees Damon. I notice the corners of Damon's mouth twitching before he breaks into a smile. "I'll never forget some of the things we did together. Remember that time, I think we were freshmen in high school, he got us organized into that '*Poler Bear Club*'? We all met down at Klode Beach to go swimming on New Year's Day?"

"Boy, I'll say I remember," booms Bearclaw, all signs of pensiveness having vanished. "I'll never forget how I felt when I hit that freezing water. He even got the local press down there to take pictures of us freezing our asses off."

"Hey look!" I say, walking to the desk to get the manila envelope full of Christopher's pictures. "I still have that picture I clipped from the newspaper of you guys jumping around in the waves." Laughter accompanies the picture as it is passed around the room.

Bearclaw's eyes narrow in serious contemplation. "Chris and I were friends since I moved here in third grade. I know he did a lot of crazy things, but there was something really deep about him. He helped me out plenty of times when I was in a tight spot. You know," he looks around the room at us as if seeking our confirmation, "he was real understanding of people when they were having a bad time."

"You're right about that," Mike agrees quickly. I noticed that more as he got older. He was always willing to help out if someone needed him."

"Yeah," Bearclaw agrees. His eyes dance as he adds with a chuckle, "Remember what a lousy baseball team we had last summer?" He and Mike played in a summer league together the last few years.

"I remember it was pretty poor," agrees Damon. "Chris and I came to watch a couple of those games."

"This one time," Bearclaw goes on, "we were losing about twenty-eight to two and Ollie comes up to me and says, 'Your team's looking real good there. All you have to do is start getting a few more hits.'"

"He was like that," says Mike. "On the surface you couldn't see what a sensitive guy he was . . . until you got to spend some time with him."

"I know that when he got older he felt sorry for teasing us girls so mercilessly," says Geri.

"I'll have to agree with you there," says Peggy.

"Remember when I graduated with my Bachelor's in Social Work and he gave me a check for one hundred dollars as a gift? When I looked surprised he said, 'That's to make up for dangling the dead mouse in your face.'"

Cathy laughs. "I loved your reply. Remember what you said? 'That's a good down payment, Chris.'"

Laughter echoes through the room. It feels good to laugh again. I search my mind for another story to tell about Chris. It seems as if we are keeping him with us a little longer by calling up these wonderful memories of his life.

Before I can think of anything Harry breaks the silence. "It doesn't seem long ago that Chris told us about his wedding plans," he says. "One day he said to me, 'It's about time I settle down. I'm not getting any younger.' He was twenty-three then. He married Karen a year later."

The familiar ache comes back into my heart. The room is quiet as each of us ponders how young Christopher was. Cathy speaks quietly, her voice gaspy as though she is about to cry. "He crowded so much into his life . . . it's as if he knew . . . as if he had some internal clock telling him he didn't have much time to fit everything in."

Unable to sleep, I lie in bed and listen to Mary's quiet footsteps going up the stairs to bed, then Mike's, then to Harry turning off the TV and coming into the bedroom. The bedsprings creak as he settles into a comfortable position. The house becomes quiet except for the gurgling and humming of the refrigerator as it goes through its middle of the night defrost cycle.

As I drift into semi-consciousness the day's events pass before me in disjointed scenes. Peter's voice crackles the microphone with sobs during his speech in church; tears stream down Uncle Ray's face as he sits near the altar in his priestly robes listening to Peter's homily—the first time I'd ever seen Uncle Ray cry. I see sunlit drops of holy water arcing through the crisp December air to anoint a rose bedecked coffin; and the last glimpse of my crystal rosary entwined through cold stiff fingers.

Suddenly I startle, fully awake, gasping for air, my body warning me that my blood oxygen saturation has dropped to an unacceptable level. My chest feels crushed. The heaviness of my losses feel like stones resting on my heart. It's the first time I decide it would be easier to die than to live. With great effort I take conscious deep breaths, struggling against the pain in my heart.

Through the blackness of this night I send up a desperate prayer. "Help me, God. I can't stand to live with this pain any more." I want to ask God to let me die but a sudden dark fear stops me. The request seems too terrible to put into words. I breathe deeply, quietly, wondering what it is I want from God. I begin to feel the emptiness about me, within me, warming with the faintest touch of Him. He comes upon me stealthily like the barely perceptible rise in humidity when a pot of water is boiling on the stove.

In His comforting presence I feel my body relaxing, my breath coming easier. Happiness is what I want. "Dear God, I want to be happy again," I tell Him simply. My prayer is soft, feathery, barely whispered. "I want us all to be happy again . . . the way we used to be."

"Yes." He touches me with His gentle self and for a brief moment I feel it . . . happiness . . . like it always was, and it is very good. Too soon the infusion of His joy begins to fade. I cling to it. I hold very still searching my thoughts, remembering how it feels to be happy, how all things were happy that last year we had together when smiles and laughter came easily.

❧ 18 ❧

The 6 O'clock News

The children and their families are gone. They've packed their belongings and gone separate ways, to assimilate alone the imprint of our newest tragedy. Two weeks have passed since Christopher died. Phone calls and sympathy cards have trailed off. In the resulting solitude Harry and I are forced to come to terms with our loss. We retreat into a semblance of routine daily living. I don't have the energy or the courage to return to work. I know I must go back soon, but not yet.

We settle in front of the TV in the family room distracting ourselves with the six o'clock news while our dinner cooks. The smoky smell of baking chicken, its fat spattering and burning on the sides of the oven, follows us from the kitchen. Harry sits next to me in his lounge chair, the ice cubes clinking against the side of his glass as he stirs his Martini. I stretch my legs out on the couch. The local news announcer on the screen peers out at us solemnly as he speaks:

"Statistics show that with the approach of the holiday season, there is an alarming increase in alcohol related deaths on our highways. Since the first of December, five young adults have lost their lives in drunk driving accidents in Milwaukee and adjacent counties. On December third, twenty-nine year old Christopher Olive was fatally injured when the car in which he was a passenger went out of control and hit a parked vehicle."

The sound of Christopher's name jolts me like a charge of electricity. I jerk forward, feet on the floor, back rigid, my entire consciousness riveted to the screen as the announcer continues his grim statistics.

"Sobriety testing proved the driver of the car to have a blood alcohol level of 0.14 at the time of the accident. He is being charged with reckless driving, speeding, and homicide by intoxicated use of a motor vehicle."

The newscaster lists the names, ages, dates, and grizzly circumstances of the other four deaths—all young men or women in their late teens or twenties. Wasted to the compelling power of alcohol.

How many times have I listened to statistics like these? Listened, shook my head, then turned away to mash the potatoes thinking, "Something's got to be done about these drunk drivers."

Now it's our turn. Our son. Not a statistic. A

precious, irreplaceable person whom we love, were sharing our lives with, our plans for the future. A child we had nurtured and known intimately for twenty-nine years. A child with whom we had dreamed many dreams. Gone without warning in the time it takes to snap your fingers.

While I listen, the other names keeps hitting me, stabbing at my heart. I feel with intense clarity the pain that is at this moment striking the loved ones of the other victims. I pull my attention from the screen to look over at Harry. He's blotting his cheeks with his handkerchief. "He was only twenty-eight," he mumbles through the cloth.

I nod. "They made a mistake." He would have been twenty-nine in another week. I'm too numb with pain to cry. We turn off the TV. We pick at our dinner in silence. Any more words about what we heard would imbed the pain more deeply into our minds and hearts.

As the days pass we slump into a pattern of silence, speaking little of Christopher's death. We haven't completed our grieving over Philip and this new loss is too much to comprehend. If I do try to make a comment about Chris, Harry says, "Just forget it. It doesn't do any good to talk about it." He pulls a shell around his grief and drinks a little more.

For a while I follow his lead, drinking brandy to numb the pain. I was never good at holding my liquor. Two glasses of brandy on ice turn the world around me into an unsteady blur. Yet, here I am in the center fully aware of my broken heart. About this time my suicide support group leader sends out a brochure to help us get through the holidays. One piece of advice hits me right between the drinks. "Don't try to drown your sorrows in alcohol. All that will do is make you a sad drunk." She is right. I would have to drink myself into unconsciousness to stop the pain.

Sometimes I try just a little brandy to relieve my indigestion. It helps at first, then starts to make my stomach burn. I'm afraid I'm getting an ulcer. Many nights I lie in bed for hours waiting for sleep to come. I try a little warmed brandy with honey to help me fall asleep. Sometimes the cozy brew puts me to sleep for a couple of hours; other times I lie awake with my head spinning and my stomach burning. I finally give up brandy entirely as a grief aid.

December 22nd approaches. . . Christopher's twenty-ninth birthday. I know I'll need help getting through this day so I plan a birthday dinner in his honor and invite all the Milwaukee-based children. Unlike my announcement of a posthumous birthday party for Philip last January, this one raises no eyebrows nor elicits any protests. Now the family understands.

When I tell Karen, she refuses to come. Her voice comes through the phone in a high pitched tremolo. "I just couldn't handle it, not yet. I already had his birthday present bought and wrapped before . . . well, you know. . . I keep looking at it."... I wait while her soft gasping sobs blow into the receiver. "What am I going to do with it now?" She breaks down and cries loudly into the phone. . . .

"I understand. But, we'll miss you. I'll keep in touch." Her refusal doesn't surprise me. I talked to her mother a few days earlier.

"We're so worried about Karen," Joanne said. "She's hardly eaten anything since Chris died. She's nothing but skin and bones, and I know she's not sleeping well. Sometimes I'm afraid she's not going to make it." I convey my own concerns about Karen to her, and suggest she might try getting Karen to see a doctor. We promise to call each other frequently.

The birthday party is a small gathering attended only by Mike, Geri, Cathy, and Peggy. We work our way through dinner with little conversation and then I light the candles on Christopher's cake. We sing 'Happy Birthday' with tears streaming down our faces. This time we don't wait for Christopher's spirit to breathe from Heaven and extinguish the flames. I lean over and blow them out myself.

I call Karen again to see if she's coming to our Christmas celebration. I reach her sister who has moved in with her to alleviate the loneliness of the house without Chris. "Karen's not home right now but I'll tell her you called." The inflection and tone of her voice sound very much like Karen.

"How is Karen doing? I talked to your Mom last week and she sounded pretty worried. She said Karen isn't eating right."

"She looks like a toothpick now. I've been doing

some cooking, coaxing her to eat, but she barely tastes anything. It's going to take her a long time to get through this. Last night when she got home from work she sat out in her car for two hours. I couldn't get her to come in. She said, 'I don't want to come into the house now that Chris isn't here.'"

"This doesn't sound good. Is there something we can do to help her? . . . or help you?"

"I don't know. Our whole family is trying to find a way to help her. We're all miserable watching her hurting like this. I'll be sure to let you know if we think of some way you can help. Do you want me to tell her you called?"

"What I called about is to invite her to our family Christmas party. She and Chris never missed it."

"I'll tell her she's invited . . . but, I don't think she'll come. It's another place where she and Chris were always together. . . and he won't be there."

"Yes. . . you're right. But I want her to know that we're thinking about her and we want her to come."

"I'll be sure and tell her." I realize now that there is nothing we can do to lessen Karen's pain. Any contact with our family will deepen her awareness of Christopher's absence. Maybe at some later date . . . I'll call again in a few months.

Our Christmas celebration seems impossible to contemplate so I make no decisions about anything. I don't even consider not celebrating this year. That would be even harder. My mind puts the whole holiday season on automatic, and in robot-like fashion I shop, wrap, decorate, cook. Everything the same, right down to the lights around the big front window and the menu for Christmas dinner. Of course, all the Christmas gift names had been drawn before Christopher died, all the gift wishes sent around, and again, as I had done after Philip's death last year, I called around to eliminate Christopher's name and gifts from the group.

When I call Mary to find out which names they drew she tells me they've changed their minds about spending the holidays with Mike's parents. "I want to spend Christmas at home, Mom. I've felt so depressed since Chris died. I mope around and cry all the time. I need to be with the family."

Petite tomboy that she was, Mary was closer to him than any of our other children, until the day she married and moved to Minnesota. Just a year and a half older than Chris she shared his zest for adventure and knack for making new and unconventional friends. As teenagers they liked the same music and took guitar lessons together. Yes. . . . . . It's not surprising that his death has flattened her usually high spirits.

Peter calls to say they'll fly home the day before Christmas. To my inquiries he tells me, yes, they're all doing okay. Jill's pregnancy, now in its sixth month is proceeding without complications. "Molly says if the baby isn't a girl we needn't bother bringing it home."

Our children don't offer to decorate the tree this year, so I begin hanging the ornaments alone. To force myself into a Christmas spirit I line up my taped Christmas carols and keep playing them over and over while I work. I lift a layer of crumpled paper and see that I've uncovered Christopher's ornaments. Floods of images fill me as I pick up his gilded reindeer with the one broken antler.

We named him Christopher which means "Christ Bearer". He was our Christmas baby bringing another helping of Christ's love into our world. Later we hear that some of Harry's relatives think it's a strange name. No one in Olive history ever had the name Christopher. He spent his first Christmas cuddled in my arms in a double room of the maternity ward; a makeshift Christmas tree on my bedside table held his special ornaments.

I untangle a spare ornament hook from the box, twist the end through the tiny gold loop on the reindeer's back, and hang it on a prominent branch. Christopher's ornaments will go up front this year.

The tone of our Christmas Day party is more melancholy than last year. Jardo, in a state of depression, decides at the last minute not to come. Even the surprise gifts stir up little gayety among the adults. Only Mike's gift to Peter, a memorial painting of Phil and Chris, sparks a temporary burst of lively conversation.

When Peter holds it up for viewing I immediately recognize the scene as my mother's Round Lake estate in Keshena. I see two small boys, one slim and blonde, the other shorter with dark hair, fishing in the reeds along the lakeshore. It takes a few seconds before the mature faces of Philip and Christopher, formed by tree branches in the hazy sky above, appear to me.

Peter studies the picture closely and starts laughing. "Look at this!" He points to the opposite shoreline which to me looks like nothing more than distant trees and brush. Jill, sitting next to him leans over his arm for a better look. She laughs too. Unable to wait till the picture gets passed to me I cross the room and peer over the top of it. With my face ten inches away I can see that the brush on the opposite shore is actually dozens of containers of plump pimento stuffed green olives, their contents spilling over onto the ground. I keep the secret and watch the smiles and giggles that break out as each one examines the picture.

We gather around the table and fold our hands as Uncle Ray leads us in prayer, He adds a special remembrance of Phil and Chris and those that have gone on ahead. We do a fair job of demolishing the turkey and trimmings. As soon as the grandchildren have helped themselves to the dessert tray of cookies and candies, they begin leaving the table and spreading out through the house. Their laughter filters through the kitchen doorway as they try out their toys. I hear the metallic clinking sounds of their new Slinky's doubling over as they make their way down the stairs. At least the children are having fun at the party.

Around the table the talk is somber. Mary is the first to bring up the subject of Christopher's death. "I dunno, Mom. This is getting scary. Every time the phone rings at home I'm afraid it's you with some more terrible news."

Cathy agrees. "I was devastated by what happened to Philip last year, but I figured it was one of those unusual tragedies that hits a family once in a lifetime. But now, this freak accident happens to Chris. I feel like this family is cursed."

Peggy nods her head prophetically as she looks at me. "First your mother dies, then fourteen months later Philip dies, then fourteen months after that Chris dies. I feel like . . . like something bad is going to happen again . . . In fourteen months someone else is going to die."

A tense silence follows while each of us considers this new threat. For years I've been the optimist in the family, the soother of fears, the fixer of feelings. But now I've lost the gift. "I'm having those thoughts too," I confess.

"I can see it in your face, Mom." Mike looks into my eyes. "You always look like you're worrying." I feel all eyes on me while I nod my head 'yes'.

Peter lets out a guttural "a huhnn." then adds, "we've been feeling kind of spooked ourselves. Things don't feel secure anymore."

I raise my shoulders in a helpless gesture. "I used to have a good feeling about life. You know, like even if the going is rough for a while, eventually everything will turn out fine."

Harry answers with a cynical laugh. "You can forget that."

The old year fades with a gloomy 'good riddance' but I look to the new one with trepidation lumping around in me, and fearful specters hiding in my corners. I'm again working full time at the hospital, but even there I can't shake my fears. I plod through each night's duties with worried feelings about what's going to happen next.

I come down with a nasty cold; or is it the flu? Everyone in the family is catching it. After two weeks of coughing and aching all over I go to the doctor. In checking me out he finds that my blood pressure is still running in the one hundred fifties over the high nineties. It has been too high since last September at which time it was diagnosed as an inner ear infection.

"Have you been getting regular exercise?" he asks me in an accusing manner. Doctors used to make me feel like a small child standing in front of a stern father. But after working alongside doctors for years I've discovered they are as vulnerable as I am.

"Plenty. . . aerobics three times a week, plus I do my own housework."

"Hmmmph," he says twisting up his stethoscope and stuffing it into the pocket of his lab coat while he considers his next move. "I'm going to have to start you on hypertensive medication. Take this once a day and come back for a checkup next week," he says scratching a few words on his prescription pad. The medication he prescribes does no good, so we experiment with different drugs till he finds the right combination to keep my blood pressure stable.

In the meantime my coughing and sneezing continue, unrelieved by the antibiotics he prescribed. At his suggestion I make an appointment with an allergist who discovers I've developed severe allergies to dust, dogs, and feathers. I begin taking a breakthrough discovery in antihistamines; one which doesn't make people drowsy. My sneezing and coughing disappear instantly. I sleep a little better now that I can breathe easily, and the blood pressure medication relaxes me. I no longer feel like a locomotive is rumbling through my body when I lie down.

In hindsight I see that I should have had a thorough check up sooner. As a nurse I know the havoc that emotions of grieving play with our bodies. Each time we are struck with the pain of remembering our loss, our cerebral cortex – the receiver/de-scrambler part of our brain – sends an alarm to our hypothalamus, our brain's relay station. Unfortunately, our hypothalamus can't distinguish between a viscous dog attack and a painful memory so it sends an alarm to our autonomic nervous system, our somatic neural efferent systems, and to our pituitary gland which activates our entire glandular system. This is the efficient 'Fright, Fight, or Flight' mechanism that saves our lives. Activated many times a day by painful memories, it can kill us.

Briefly: it make our hearts beat faster, enlarges heart and lung blood vessels, while constricting blood flow to our skin, reproductive, and digestive organs. This call to action increases the rate and depth of our respirations to get more oxygen to our brain and skeletal muscles. It increases sweating—our body's cooling system—and begins to break down proteins stored in our liver converting them to glucose for quick energy.

Scientifically, I know all this, but being a stubborn individual I wanted to handle my painful emotions in my own way. There's a rumor in healthcare that doctors and nurses make the worst patients. "They always think they know what's best for themselves." That rumor is ninety-nine point nine per cent true.

"Mom, I've been noticing something about you," Cathy confronts me one day.

"What's that?"

"You cried all the time after Philip died. I've hardly seen you cry at all since Chris died."

I feel compelled to defend myself. "I realize that. I don't know why I'm not crying more. It isn't that I didn't love Chris as much. I guess I'm just tired. . . too tired, and too depressed to cry."

I start to worry about why I don't cry about Christopher. I call Bill to discuss it with him. "I had a lot of guilt feelings when Philip died, like I was in some way responsible for his death. Maybe that's why I cried more when he died. There was nothing I could do to prevent Christopher's death."

"That's very true, but that isn't why you're not crying about Christopher. You've been under tremendous stress for over a year. You're emotionally exhausted. You haven't yet begun dealing with your grief over Chris. It's going to take time."

His words make sense and some part of me knows they're true, but I resist them. "Bill, I don't want to go on grieving. I'm sick and tired of being sad. Isn't there some way I can get over this?"

"There is no way to rush through this. It will probably be a matter of years before you've dealt with all your grieving."

At his words I feel my chest cave. My heart feels like a rock in quicksand. "This is too hard," I murmur, my voice barely audible.

"I know," he says gently. "I've been praying for you. Remember, I told you I'm available any time during the day or night. Be sure to call me when you need support." He pauses while I tell him I will call. "And keep writing about your feelings. That's something that might help you work through this a little faster."

❧ 19 ❧

Heaven's View

Six weeks after Christopher's death, I kneel in the same church in which his funeral was held, at a memorial liturgy being said for him at the request of my friends. When the celebrant approaches the altar I see it is the same priest that concelebrated his Funeral Mass with Uncle Ray. An unthinking reflex directs my vision to the central spot in the aisle where the casket stood. A conviction hits me like a brand new revelation, "Christopher is dead!" Fresh grief rises up from some dormant place to reactivate my emotions and release my tears.

As the liturgy progresses I blot my eyes and wipe my nose while I attempt to concentrate on the prayers. In the benches ahead of me are school children that I judge to be about third grade level. They are meticulously lined up and evenly spaced. Their teachers kneel behind them overseeing their every move. I can tell that the children have helped prepare this liturgy by its appealing simplicity appropriate for nine year-olds. The unaffected joy of their songs and scripture readings begins carrying me along. The sadness in my heart grows lighter.

When we get to the central part of the service, the priest stretches out his arms and prays, "Remember, oh Lord, those who have gone before us with the sign of faith in the hope of rising again, especially Christopher Olive for whom this Mass is being celebrated. Admit him and all the faithful departed into the presence of your glory."

At these words a stream of joy passes through me filling me with a warm sense of Christopher's presence. He is intensely happy and I seem to hear his voice saying. "You should see how neat this looks from up here." He conveys to me a small portion of the glory he is receiving and tells me not to be sad anymore. "We'll all be together soon and our adventures will be even better than before." Throughout the remainder of the service I can feel his presence and his joy. It's typical 'Christopher joy' accompanied by the thrill of excitement he so loved on earth.

When the service ends I leave church and with it his presence, but the happiness I've received stays with me for several days. When the pleasant emotions fade, I try vainly to prolong them by thinking of Christopher and his liturgy. But grief's time must be served, and sorrow moves back in on me no matter what tactics I use to evade it. The only difference is that now I can cry. It's a tremendous relief.

Philip's birthday comes around again, the second one since he died. I call Sue to tell her about the plans I've made for that day. "I'm having a memorial Mass said for him at seven o'clock in the morning and then I was hoping we could meet for lunch somewhere."

"I'll meet you for lunch, but I don't know about making it to your church at seven. I'll see what I can do."

I kneel at the early morning liturgy supposedly wrapped in prayer, but actually pondering what Philip would look like on his thirty-fifth birthday. Sue slides into the pew next to me. "I'm on my way to work but I didn't want to miss this," she whispers. I turn my head enough to give her a grateful smile. It feels good to have her next to me. After Mass we light vigil lights in front of the white marble 'Pieta' at a side altar. It has become my favorite statue.

Later she comes from work to meet me for lunch at a nearby restaurant. Harry, Mike, Cathy, and Peggy join us. Sue brings some old letters of Philip's to share with us, and over coffee or cokes, we take turns reading them. We talk about him and remember the good old days and the fun things we did with him. It's a good birthday remembrance, but in the midst of our conversation and laughter, I can discern the unremitting ache in my heart. That night I write a sad poem in my journal:

"My sorrow is a vine that winds and twists through
all my thoughts of memories passed,
Through daily chores and quiet bits of gentle
conversations,

Through happy celebrations big and small and
Through the joyous Christmas feasts and fun of
summer camping trips,
Through times alone with Harry, reminiscing.

My sorrow is a vine that sends out shoots for me to
see and feel whichever way I turn.
Come now, oh God, to pluck away this vine so I can
serve you as you wish in peaceful joy and love."

He answers me.
"Not even I, your God, can take this vine away from
you,
For it is so entwined through your whole growth of
life.
If I uproot the vine it will destroy your life as well.

So I must let it stay until the harvest.
Then I will tear it out and cast it off from you.
In heaven you'll recall the vine, but without pain,
and with a greater joy for having borne it."

How many times a day does a mother think of
her children? That many times I remember that
Philip and Christopher are dead and the pain begins
anew. Christopher's death has exacerbated my
feelings of loss over Philip and I'm again grieving
heavily for him. I find that I can never grieve for
both of the children at the same time. Sometimes I
cry with the fresh pangs of grief for Christopher, at
other times the familiar ache of longing for Philip
takes over.

I get no happiness from old pleasures that used to entice me . . . going to a movie with Geri and sharing a box of popcorn; curling up for an hour with a favorite book; a bowl of chocolate peanut butter custard from our nearby drive-in. Not even family celebrations or partying with friends makes me happy. The familiar trappings of daily life seem incredibly dull. Talking on the phone with Judie one day I find myself saying, "I'd give everything I own to have my boys back again." Later I think about what I said. Would I really? Absolutely.

Except for family gatherings I avoid social events as much as possible. Not only do I feel too exhausted to dress up and go out, I also feel like a pariah among my friends. I pummeled them last year with accounts of Philip's death, and this year with Christopher's. They have troubles of their own and don't need to keep listening to mine. And I can't seem to talk with them the way I used to. I find it tedious taking part in everyday chitchat. I feel irritated when I have to listen to it.

I accept one social invitation. Bill gives a going away party for our friend, Paul Roche, a scholar and poet who made our acquaintance during his year teaching poetry and Greek drama at the university. He's a person of exceptional learning and talent, a man possessed of a deep, mystical wisdom. He's heard about my loss of another son and offers his sympathy. He holds my hand, his blue eyes shining intently. "There's a plan for all of this, you know. These difficulties don't come upon us by accident."

His words unlock a truth I have held on to in a

deep subconscious plane. "Yes. Yes, I believe that's true."

Paul presents me with an unpublished poem he has written. "Perhaps this will help you." I thank him and take refuge in a quite corner of the house to read it.

THOSE WHOM THE GODS LOVE
(Elegy for a young man killed in a car crash)
Come Death, let us leave,
you and I together.
I would sooner leave alive
than have you gather

A bag of slowly moving bones
arthritic and distressed.
So take me dancing sarabands,
stately, perfect, dressed

In dalmatics of gold and all my prime
with every limb in flower.
Thus let me go before my time
and not dismissed
Clinging to every second in the hour.

Shall we not tread beyond
whatever grim horizon
Hides me from the sun?
So walk me hand in hand
To a land I have my eyes on.

Come Death, let us leave,
you and I together.

As I contemplate his words, I feel as if scattered pieces of a puzzle are settling into place. This tragic moment in time makes no sense to me now, but I believe it will. God is in control and his master plan is sound.

By the time I reach home another truth has become clear to me. Death is not good. Death was not part of God's original plan. Something has gone wrong with us—terribly wrong. What we are seeing now is God's contingency plan for setting things right. I recall the joyful words of twelfth century mystic, Julian of Norwich, as she quotes God's promise to her, "I can make all things well, I shall make all things well, and you shall see that every kind of thing will be well." The days and weeks that follow seem less heavy, a bit more bearable with this glimmer of hope shining through them.

"Remember how I told you I kept seeing Philip all over the university after he died?" Peggy asks me one day. I tell her I do. "Well, now I'm seeing Chris all over the place. Mom, I had no idea so many people look like him."

"Well, now that you mention it, I've been seeing him drive by in his gray Toyota. . . A young man with dark wavy hair, parted in the middle, the neat black mustache, and those oversized sunglasses he always wore while driving."

Cathy and Mike discuss their sightings of him, the most frequent vision being the one of him driving by in his Toyota. "It's just a coincidence," says Mike. "That Toyota is a popular car right now and

Chris had that typical 'Yuppie' look with his hair parted in the middle, the mustache and sunglasses."

"Well, maybe," says Cathy, her face screwed up in a doubtful frown.

Later in the week I sit through an entire luncheon with Harry, staring across the restaurant at the back of a man's head . . . a head with dark brown wavy hair shaped like Christopher's. A man just the right height, muscular shoulders, a hint of a mustache visible when he turns his head slightly. I keep looking up from my plate, anxious for him to turn around. If Harry notices my furtive glances, he doesn't say anything. What am I looking for? Even if the man looks exactly like Chris it won't be him. That doesn't matter. I'm so hungry for the sight of him I keep my watch. When at last the young man rises and turns toward me I'm disappointed. His eyes are too small and his nose and lips too pudgy. Not at all like Christopher.

My journal begins filling with more and more reflections about Christopher. I want to remember every detail about him. I decide to write down his entire life's story. I take refuge in the second floor spare bedroom writing for hours at a time, oblivious of my body or my environment. Sometimes the memories make me cry but I keep on typing, swiping across my face with a tissue.

By March I've assembled Christopher's biography and am making a final draft when Peter calls. "It's a boy. A big healthy one. We're naming him Jeffrey Christopher, the second name in memory of Chris." . . . "Yes, Jill is fine too. Eddie is thrilled to have a little brother." . . . "I don't care what Molly says, we're bringing him home."

This news enhances my pleasure at having recorded Christopher's story. When Jeffrey Christopher is older he can read the story about 'Uncle Chris' after whom he is named. Giving copies of the biography to all the children and to Karen feels extremely satisfying. I have saved Chris for them; saved him from extinction.

Next I begin on Philip's life story. It's more painful to recall his life. There are conflicts here I haven't finished resolving. I've been skipping my suicide group meetings so I can spend all of my spare time writing. With what I've learned from them I'm able to view Philip's suicide more realistically. As I write I see that I'm emphasizing the trouble spots in our relationship. After I have them down on paper and read them over I realize much of it is normal parent/child conflict, the same things our other children lived through. I toss some of the stickier recollections into the wastebasket.

Harry interrupts one of my writing sessions to tell me I have a phone call. It's Joanne calling to tell me how much she enjoyed Christopher's biography. "We keep it out on our coffee table. The whole family is reading it." In answer to my inquiries she tells me that Karen is eating more and getting a full night's sleep. "She's beginning to fill out a little. Did she tell you that we planted a tree in memory of Christopher next to our summer home on the Mississippi?"

"No, I haven't talked with her lately. But, what a beautiful thing to do."

"It was beautiful. He and Karen had so much fun at the river she wanted something there to remember him by. She used some of the memorial gifts we received at the funeral services to buy it. We all helped to dig the hole or carry water. We cried a lot while we were working, but it was good. It feels like we have a little bit of Chris still with us. She wants to plant a tree for him at Judie and Jardo's farm. They spent a lot of time there too."

"That's a wonderful idea. I'm going to give Karen a call and see what kind of arrangements she's made. I'd like our whole family to be there for the planting." When I call Karen she tells me Jardo has put in an order for a flowering crab tree but no definite date has been set for the planting.

"Jardo says we have to wait and find out when the tree can be delivered. He'll let you know in plenty of time to get the family up there. Also, I've been wanting to call and tell you about Kenny. You know, the guy that caused Christopher's accident?"

"Oh, yes. I'd forgotten about him. Is he serving time?"

"Nothing's happened to him yet. He's still out on bail. He hired a lawyer who keeps finding ways to delay the hearing. I'm getting kind of mad about it. I thought they would have locked him up by now."

"Yes. I thought it would be an easy conviction. He's obviously guilty. If you hear any more about him let me know." Karen promises to call when she learns more about Ken.

"That's a great idea," says Mike when I tell him about planting memorial trees for Christopher. The whole family gets excited about a tree planting at the farm. But Jardo calls to say the flowering crab tree is back-ordered and can't be delivered in time for this year's planting season.

"They have to be planted in March or April as soon as the ground thaws and before the sap starts running. We've decided to put it on hold till next Spring." Were disappointed to have to wait so long, but we set a tree planting date for the second last week of April next year.

"I've got some new pieces hanging in the student exhibit at the Fine Arts Gallery," Mike tells us. "Be sure to get over to see them, Mom, I think you'll like them."

I make my way to the university's fine arts building on my next day off. After browsing through the large student exhibit room and winding my way slowly along the walkways examining the sculptures and paintings, I come to a smaller adjoining display room. A large work takes up an entire wall and I know at once it is Mike's. A full-sized horizontal figure shrouded in a black winding sheet is being lowered into a grave. The figure emerges from the canvas several inches giving it a life-like (or death-like) appearance. Falling into the grave and lying at the bottom in broken angles are the gloves. Dozens of dark dirty gloves, crushed, smashed, their fingers and thumbs bent off in unnatural positions. Dead gloves, being discarded into their final resting place.

I walk forward for a closer look. Black four-inch tiles line the grave; on each is a faint life drawing hinting at a being engaged in the lively pursuits of an active lifestyle. Christopher's life.

I stand before the picture crying silently. When I turn to go I nearly bump into the sculpture behind me. I see it's entitled 'Baptismal Font' by Michael Olive. Curious. It appears to be made of carved concrete and stands as high as my shoulders resting on a base designed of zigzagging pieces of wood. I peer over the edge of the concrete basin and see it is filled with water. My breath catches in my throat. Under the surface of the water I see a plaster cast of Philip's face staring up at me, broken into several pieces lying a bit separate from each other; the broken body and spirit of my precious child.

As soon as I get back home I call Mike. "Your art pieces are amazing. I've worked for months putting my feelings about Phil and Chris into words. I've filled up hundreds of pages. You have grasped them perfectly in your two works of art."

Like me, Peggy has worked through her grief in writing. She's well into the first semester of her Master's program and she's going for a minor in psychology. One of her electives is a class on death and dying. She shares with us a paper she's written about grieving for a class assignment. In it she describes our dreams about her deceased brothers.

"Bargaining, as a stage of grief, is useless once someone we love dies. Reason tells us we can't cut any deals that will bring a person back to life. My family and I continue to bargain for my brothers' lives in dreams. I found my brother, Philip, alive and well in my dream, living in my parents house. The catch was he could remain alive and well only if he never left the house. My sister Cathy dreamed he was living incognito in an apartment near the university and could only come home for short visits. My mother reports the strangest dream. Philip was with us but we could only see him reflected in mirrors. She took us all to a department store dressing room where we stood in front of the triple mirrors to visit with him.

"After my brother Chris died mom dreamed that he showed up casually one day and told her the doctors tried a new medication that brought him back to life. My dream about Chris topped them all. I ran into him in an Eastside bar. He explained to me that he was working for the CIA and his death was staged to throw off enemy agents.

"As silly as these dreams seem on awakening, they serve to release some of the tension of grieving while we sleep. And as a bonus, we get to see and hear our brothers just as they were, one more time."

The dreams Peggy describes in her paper continue, the most frequent dreamers being Peggy, Cathy, Sue and myself. Sue continues to dream about Philip, while Peggy, Cathy, and I alternate between Philip and Chris. They are all hokey, impossible dreams in which one or the other boys is able to come back to us. While we are dreaming them, they seem entirely plausible. When we exchange dream stories later we laugh about them. In comparing dreams we discover that no one ever dreams about both of the boys appearing in the same dream. Geri complains that she never dreams about either one of them. "It would be good to see and hear them again, if only in a dream."

Karen calls to tell me, "Yesterday I talked to one of Christopher's former co-workers at the court house. He filled me in on what's happening with Kenny's drunk driving charge."

"Oh, yes. I've been wondering about that. Have they got the case wrapped up yet?"

"No. He and his lawyer are still dragging it out. The lawyer found a mistake on the records with the blood alcohol level. Somebody typed in the wrong time for when the test was supposed to have been taken, so this lawyer is trying to get it thrown out as evidence."

"That's ridiculous. Sounds like it was just a typo."

"It was." Her voice becomes louder. I hear her anger. "But his lawyer started an appeal to get it dismissed from the records. The appeal process will take three to six months."

"I can't believe they'll be able to get the blood alcohol level thrown out as evidence."

"My Dad's lawyer says there's not much of a chance. What makes me mad is the way they're dragging this out. When the appeal process is finished they have to schedule another court hearing. That could take a couple more months. I'm anxious to get this whole thing over with so I can put it out of my mind."

"That's for sure. So what's happening to Kenny in the meantime?"

"He's out on bail, going about business as usual. They're even letting him drive a car to work and back." She sounds close to tears. "It isn't fair."

"Absolutely not fair. Kenny is clearly guilty, and I don't like the idea of him driving before this is settled. Also, I've been wondering, will this delay hold up payment of damages from the accident?"

"There's no problem with that. No matter what Ken's conviction is, his auto insurance has to cover everything. They're even picking up all the funeral expenses. We're making them pay for everything, the flowers, the buffet dinner after the funeral, the whole works."

"I'm glad you're having them pay for those funeral expenses. I never would have thought of that."

"Well that's my job you know. I've been working for insurance companies since I graduated from high school. Besides, my Dad's lawyer has been going over all the technicalities with us so we don't fall through any legal loopholes. Financially, I'm in good shape. Chris left a big insurance policy, enough to pay off our mortgage, but I'm not sure if I want to do that. Maybe I won't stay here."

"I can understand that." I feel relieved that she's thinking through her problems and looking to the future. She's going to make it through this. "Take your time about making those decisions, there's no . . ."

"Oh, before I forget," she interrupts. "I want to give you my new phone number. I got it changed the other day." I grab the pen off our notepad holder by the phone and write down the number she gives me. "Ever since the article about the accident appeared in the paper I've been getting lots of phone calls. Not just from friends either. Some of them are salesmen; that's not so bad. But there are weird ones too. Odd religious messages. And the worst one was from a man who said he was a lonely widower. I think he was trying to hit on me. It's getting spooky so I'm keeping this new number unlisted."

❧ 20 ❧

New Life

Together, and yet apart, we grieve our way through the somber season of Lent . . . forty days for reflecting on the deeper meanings of life and death. Our Wisconsin weather sets the right mood by providing plenty of damp, dreary days. Sunshine is rare. I don't burden myself with more prayer or fasting. Life has dumped enough atonement on me to inter body and soul.

Geri loads me with an extra measure of penance by announcing that she's moving. Seems her friend Kerry has been after her to join her out on Long Island . . . a New York adventure.

"I can't believe you're moving so far away. Are you sure you won't change your mind?" I'm making a last plea. It's seven in the morning. We're standing on Geri's front porch amid her suitcases and her boxes encircled with heavy twine. We wait for her friend to pick her up for the drive out to Mitchell Airport.

"I can't believe I'm doing this either, Mom." Her

mouth moves into an unconvincing smile. "But I'm getting into a rut staying here, and well . . . Kerry's got that big apartment to share and . . . you know I've always wanted to see New York."

"Are you sure you'll be able to get a job in New York?" Geri has finally accumulated enough credits to get an Associate Degree in Registered Nursing and has passed her state boards.

"Kerry says that'll be no problem. They're crying for nurses out there." She searches my eyes with her gaze. "I feel bad leaving you and Dad though, so soon after Christopher's accident."

"We're doing fine," I say firmly. I don't want her worrying about us while she's away. "I've been feeling better now that I'm only working three nights a week. And my new blood pressure medication makes me feel more relaxed. And Dad . . I don't know what he's feeling. He's not as crabby as he used to be, but he won't talk about Chris or Phil anymore. He won't even read the biographies I wrote about them."

She shakes her head, measures her words carefully. "It seems to me he's using ineffective coping mechanisms."

"I agree. All I can do is keep encouraging him to verbalize his feelings." We both smile. We have fun spoofing our profession by talking like a couple of nursing care plans.

At the sound of the car horn she hugs me one last time. Sadly I stand at the curb and wave till she's out of sight. I feel like crying. "It's not like she's dying" I tell myself sternly. "I'll see her again in a few months."

As Easter Sunday approaches, winter loosens its frost-fingered grip on our Midwestern State. I'm awakened early by the delicate trilling of a robin singing outside my bedroom window. Suddenly fascinated that so small a creature can make such a resounding melody, I hold very still and listen. I wonder why he sings so cheerily as he awakens to a chilly, uncertain dawn. More bird songs begin filtering through the half-inch opening at the bottom of my window—the chirping of sparrows, the distant squawking of crows and jays. Funny, I haven't heard the birds before today. They must have been out there.

Deciding to go to early morning church services, I slip out of bed and gather up my clothes being careful not to awaken Harry. He doesn't go to church anymore. I open the front door slowly to keep it from creaking. A cool gust of green spring air rushes in to finger my face and riffle my hair. It smells of new grass and hardy spring flowers. On the way to church I stop the car to stare at a profusion of deep purple crocuses nestling in a neighbor's front lawn. When did they start blooming? I drive on and spot the fat robin redbreast, and then a row of lemon yellow daffodils ruffling in the breeze. The sky is overcast, but not dark. The kind of checkered hazy white that lets you know the clouds will be breaking up soon. My five senses pick up delightful new messages and wing them to my brain. By the time I'm kneeling in church I tingle with joy. "Thank you God for the beauty of your creation."

Easter Sunday is the beginning of healing. With the blossoming of tulips, fruit trees, and magnolias, I feel an awakening of new life. Grief has gone out of our bleeding hearts this spring. They please me with memories of Philip's love in planting them.

The weather warms; the sun shines. I get out in my garden to weed and plant. Harry gets out his spade and turns over the soil in his tomato and cucumber patches. Sometimes I sit in the sunshine enjoying the colorful blooming and fragrance of my lilacs and my roses. At other times I watch the ants busily pushing up grains of sand through the cracks between the patio blocks. I imagine their labyrinth tunnels expanding underneath. I discover in new dimensions how beautiful life is; how fragile, how precious, is every living thing.

Summer passes quietly. We don't attempt a family camping trip this year. No one even brings up the subject. The children look a little happier and Cathy has her ulcer under control. I sense that we're all resting and recovering.

About the middle of July Karen calls to report on the progress of Kenny's conviction for drunk driving. "The judge in Madison overruled the appeal to throw out the blood alcohol level as evidence."

"Good. What happens next?"

"They're scheduling a new hearing in the Court House. The exact date isn't set yet because they're backlogged. I'll let you know when I hear."

" . . . and Kenny?"

"Still out on bail."

"And still driving, I suppose."

"That's right. It isn't fair. It shouldn't be legal."

"And they call this the 'Justice' system. It sounds like life is going on as usual for him. But, I wonder if this is bothering him. He must feel guilty, or at least worried. I'd like to be at that next hearing so I can get a look at him; see how he's handling all this. I've never laid eyes on him."

"I'm planning on going too. Maybe we can drive down together. We'll make plans as soon as I find out the date."

While I'm waiting to hear from her we receive a letter from Geri. It's good news:

"Guess what? Kerry has been transferred to a brokerage in Minneapolis. She's very happy about it because she doesn't get along with the people she works with on Wall Street. She's wrapping things up and we'll be leaving in two weeks. I'll spend a week in Milwaukee getting all my furniture together while Kerry finds us an apartment in the 'Miniapple'.

"I'm glad to be getting out of New York. It was fun for a while but most of the people here are too unfriendly. They're always in a hurry. Remember that assertiveness training we had in nursing school? Well, everybody's gone overboard with assertiveness out here on the East Coast. It's too much for a couple of timid Midwestern girls. Minneapolis sounds just right to me."

It's August before I hear from Karen about the trial. She gives me the date, time, and name of the judge who'll be hearing the case. "I've decided to drive right to the court house from work. It'll be faster for me. Oh, one more thing. The court secretary told me to call the morning of the trial. She warned me that these trials are always getting postponed and switched around right up to the last minute. You'd better call too."

Cathy and Mike are free that day and plan to go with me. We talk about Kenny and what we think the outcome of this trial should be. "I believe there must be some punitive action taken against him," I tell the others. "If only as an example to the rest of the community. But, sitting in prison for years seems too harsh."

"He'd come out worse after prison," agrees Cathy. "Maybe a suspended driver's license and some kind of community action."

"Wait a minute! Don't be so easy on the guy," says Mike. "Don't forget what he did to Chris. He deserves a prison term." Peter agrees with Mike that Kenny should do time in prison, but the rest of the family sides with me.

My attitudes are entangled with my memories of Christopher's drunk driving arrest. His friend Lars could have been killed that day, and Chris would be the one standing trial. Christopher was a dumb kid, inexperienced with the deadly effects of drinking and driving. I can't help feeling the same way about Kenny, even though Kenny was a little older and should have been wiser. So far in my grieving, I'm not aware of any angry feelings toward Kenny for his role in killing Christopher.

At my support group we talked about 'forgiving'. It's a big hurdle to cross, especially when another person, or group of persons, is clearly responsible for the death. It seems impossible to forgive when an intentional, vicious attack ends the life of someone we love. But, deliberately nursing anger at others erects a roadblock in our healing process. One of our group members has been mired in anger for years. She continually threatens suicide. Perhaps the only solution lies in consistently placing the subject of our anger into the hands of the One who unlocks the secret tangles of all hearts.

Some of us write letters to the judge letting him know our feelings in the matter. The court secretaries tell us, "Yes, the judges want to hear the views of the parties involved." and "Yes, it does influence the verdict and sentencing."

I call the courthouse the morning of the trial. The trial has been postponed. It's Ken's lawyer again. He found another loophole with which to delay the proceedings. We're all disappointed. Karen is outraged. "I've got to get this over with so I can put it out of my mind."

Unseasonably warm September nights send the crickets around our neighborhood into long stretches of frantic chirping, or whatever it is crickets do to send their vibrant music into the night air. As soon as the sky grows dusky, hundreds of them begin their concerts. I never paid much attention to crickets before, but now they fascinate me. Some nights I lie in bed trying to stay awake until they get tired and stop singing. I always fall asleep before they do.

On one of these nights a cricket with a startlingly shrill song stations himself outside my bedroom window. This unexpected, personalized serenade delights me. I marvel that this insignificant insect is a work of God's hands and is filled with a spark of His own beauty; that this 'bug' must be sustained from moment to moment by an act of His will. My cricket sings to me for four nights before moving on.

Summer's healing is insidiously interrupted when I happen to glance at an ad for the Holy Hill Craft Fair in our church bulletin. A prick of my conscience brings back Philip's words as he invites me to attend that Fair, an invitation he extended not once, but many times. I was always too busy to attend. I brush the thorn of remorse away and concentrate on the pleasantries of our warm Fall weather. The imbedded irritation grows more intense. Harry looks startled when I snap at him, or worse, becomes angry when I stare past him into space as he talks to me.

Old scenes I replayed after Philip's death come back to haunt me and I chastise myself bitterly for the wrongs I inflicted on him. Again my mind searches for scenarios I could have changed, interventions I could have used to save him. Sue calls to invite me to a memorial service she has arranged for him at Holy Hill on September twenty-fifth. The second one since he died. I tell her I will definitely attend.

On our way up to the great church on the hilltop, I tell her the regrets I'm having about never joining Philip at the annual craft show. "He worked so hard setting up that show I wish I would have taken the time to see it."

Sue gives me a long knowing look. "It's a funny thing but that craft show sent me back into the old guilt feelings I've had about Phil. He always wanted me to work there with him . . . but I was always too busy. I'll never forget that last craft fair, the one right before he died. He was there all day working, and he came home in the evening so drunk he could hardly stand. That was when I made up my mind to confront him about his drinking. It wasn't long after that I told him I couldn't live with him drinking. It was the last night . . . well, you know. . .

After the church service I drop Sue off at her house and drive over to Saint Francis Cemetery. I've brought flowers to put on Philip's grave. The sky is turning salmon pink by the time I turn into the small road that enters the cemetery. I come to a halt near the pine trees sheltering his grave. I've just begun to slide out of my car when I hear the shrill chirping of a cricket. Its untimely song surprises me for the sky has not yet darkened.

As I near Philip's grave I'm amazed to hear the cricket song coming from the depths of grass in front of his headstone. I bend down to peer into the long, untrimmed growth, but I can't see the tiny creature. When I straighten up I realize that there's no sound of chirping crickets anywhere else in the cemetery. Only one cricket . . . for me and Phil.

Entombed remorse comes pouring out in my tears as I place my flowers next to the cricket in front of Philip's headstone. I know God has arranged this private serenade to heal and comfort me, to assure me he has not forgotten my heart's pain. He is here in this tiny creature telling me He is with Philip, and Philip is with Him. I kneel on top of Philip's grave for a long time and cry with gratitude. My tears release the pain that's been trapped inside.

The leaves are glorious in their golds, reds, and orange hues before they fall, shrivel, and crunch under my feet. By mid-November the trees are black skeletons with crooked limbs and the air is damp and chilly. My spirit sinks into dreariness with the darkening days. I flip over the calendar to its last page and stare at it. December. December is Christopher's month, coming as it does with the flood of memories of his life and death.

I prepared for the first anniversary of his death by requesting a Mass said in his honor on that day. Remembering the joy I experienced at his memorial service last January, my spirit eagerly awaits the day, expecting to feel him near and happy. I invite the family to come, and Michael and Cathy attend the early morning service with me. I follow along with the prayers and I think about Chris, but no joy comes.

When the priest holds up the cup of wine, the blood of Christ, I receive a strong visual image of

Christopher's blood dripping from the gauze bandage at the back of his head, the drops forming a widening pool on a shiny table. I am struck with the horror of Christopher's death as scenes of that night in the emergency room replay in my mind. During the Communion service my thoughts are awash with blood. Blood filling us, sustaining us, running out of us when we die. I spend the rest of the day distraught and miserable.

Grief that I thought was put to rest renews its attack. I wonder how the pain can feel so fresh now that it's a year old. I know I ought to call Karen and see how she's doing, but I'm reluctant to talk to her. Chris ought to be with her, and he's not there. I call Bill to tell him something has gone wrong with me. "I felt so good all summer and now I've plunged right back into Christopher's death."

"I thought you'd be calling around the anniversary of his death." His voice is comforting and I'm immediately glad I called him. "You couldn't handle all of your grieving until you became stronger. You rested this summer and now you can tolerate these emotions. Your buried grief is surfacing. Remember, I told you this was going to take time."

I tell him I remember. "You don't think I'm morbid or unbalanced, then . . . going through all of Christopher's dying again?"

"Not at all. You've suffered massive emotional wounds. Even though you can't see them they're every bit as real as physical wounds. And they take just as long, if not longer, to heal." His words help me relax even though I don't appreciate what he's telling me.

"This grieving business . . . it takes a hell of a long time. Am I really going to get over it?"

I would have liked hearing a strong 'Yes' to that question, but Bill gives me a cautious and truthful reply. "There will probably always be some residual sadness. We never quite get over the death of our loved ones. I still think of my Grandmother dying many years ago, and I feel sad."

The weeks of December are a reluctant preparation for the holidays. Before them comes the sorrowful day that once was Christopher's happy birthday. As I had done last year I invite the family over for dinner and cake. It's a small party with Geri living in Minneapolis and the other out of town children too busy to drive so far. Sue takes time out from her busy schedule to come with Josh and Sarah.

Mike and Janel, have picked this day to have their first baby. It's her due date and she's been laboring through the night. Today her doctor has begun inducing her with an oxytocin to intensify her contractions. Both she and Mike (and the rest of us also) would like their baby to be born on Christopher's birthday. Mike calls throughout the day to keep us informed of her progress. "The Pitocin drip is keeping the contractions regular," he tells us about noon. By the time I'm putting the roast in the oven he tells me, "The doctor just put in an Epidural and right away the contractions got stronger. It shouldn't be too long now."

We sit down to the birthday dinner with solemn faces, thinking about Christopher, wishing he were here. After the main meal I bring out the cake and set it in the middle of the table. It's decorated with our old yellow plastic 'Happy Birthday' sign with 'Christopher' spelled out below it in green jelly squeezed from a tube. We're just about to light the candles and sing Happy Birthday when the phone rings. "It's a boy!" Mike's excited words come through the wire loud and clear.

"Did you hear that?" I shout to the others around the table. "It's a boy." Then back into the phone I say, "Is he healthy? How's Janel?"

"They're both doing fine. He's a big baby, ten pounds and thirteen ounces."

"Almost eleven pounds!" I cry out.

"He's got blond hair and doesn't look like either one of us. We're naming him Matthew Perry. I've got to go now. They're taking Janel to her room." I hang up the phone and dash to the cupboard to grab a plastic tube of pink jelly. I haven't got any blue. I spell out 'and Mathew' on the cake under Christopher's name.

The news of Matthew's birth changes our mood instantly from gloom to excitement. We light the candles and sing loudly, first to Chris, then to Matthew. While cake is passed around, we laugh and talk about the great coincidence of a new boy on this particular day. Someone to replace Christopher? No. But someone who will help fill the hole he left behind.

✖ 21 ✖

Fourteen Month Phobia

Christmas feels gayer this year with a new baby to shower gifts on. But still, through all the merriment there is an undercurrent of yearning for our two missing children. We roll over into the new year mixed in this unsettling paradox of happiness and sorrow.

Mike and Janel move to a new house, an easy ten minute drive from our house. I volunteer for frequent baby sitting sessions. When I hold blonde-haired baby Matthew in my arms I look down into eyes as blue as Philip's. But his husky build, squirming mass of energy and ready smiles are Christopher through and through.

Harry is enamored of his new grandson. I laugh to see him down on his hands and knees cooing and shaking rattles at little Matthew propped up in his infant seat. Mike, a bachelor for thirty-two years, surprises us by his display of competent fatherly devotion. In two weeks he has mastered the arts of diapering, bottle feeding, and burping.

Life goes along on this up and down roller-coaster fashion until the middle of January when the twinges of anxiety that pinch at my stomach become too strong to ignore. I jump with any unexpected noise, especially the sound of the telephone ringing. Cleaning up the breakfast dishes one morning I drop the butter dish when the family room wall phone rings.

"Hi, it's Cathy," the voice on the line says.

"Cathy. You startled me. Is everything okay?"

"So you're doing it too. That's what I called about."

"What do you mean? Doing what?"

"Panicking whenever the phone rings. Mom, I feel really scared. I have this sick feeling that somebody is going to die again."

"Oh my God. That's it! Fourteen months! At the end of January it will be fourteen months since Christopher died."

"That's exactly what I've been thinking.

"No wonder I feel so jumpy." I reach over for a kitchen chair and pull it toward me. Suddenly I feel too tired to hold up my own weight. "I've been waking up at night with anxiety attacks. I couldn't figure out why. Everything in my life. . . in all of our lives, is going fine." I pause a moment wondering if I should try to reassure her. "Cathy, this nervousness we're feeling, well, that doesn't mean something bad is really going to happen."

"That's what I keep telling myself. My body doesn't believe it, especially my ulcer."

"That's been acting up again? Have you been to

the doctor?"

"Oh, sure. I make regular visits. Now he says it's a duodenal ulcer. I'm taking Tagamet and antacids."

"Oh, Cathy," I breathe out the words with a long sigh, "I'm sorry. I wish there was some way I could help. Is Peggy okay?"

"She's got another cold, or flu, or something. She's been to the doctor, too. He put her on antibiotics. We talked about this fourteen month phobia, and she has a gut feeling something will happen. She says she's just waiting for the axe to fall."

"Maybe it would help if we got together. I was thinking of having a dinner on Philip's birthday. Just something quiet with the family."

"Gee, Mom, I'm afraid I can't. I have to work that night." Cathy has a new job as Respiratory Therapist at a local hospital. "Anyway I can't eat anything I like. No chocolate or coffee, nothing spicy, no soda or alcohol. I'm on a really boring diet. But I'll pass the invitation on to Peggy."

Now anxiety has a name. 'Fourteen Month Phobia'. I'm no less afraid. I call Minneapolis to ask Geri if she's feeling it. She says she hasn't felt any anxiety and reassures me that nothing bad is going to happen. I rationalize that she is right, that we've spooked ourselves into this and it's all in our minds.

Fighting with my feelings only intensifies my fear. It becomes unbearable. My body reacts with stomach cramps, diarrhea, and sleeplessness. Lying in bed one night ominous parodies on Poe's 'Raven' begin running through my head. "Nevermore,

nevermore. Will we find a bright tomorrow? Quoth the Raven 'Nevermore'. Will we ever all be happy? Quoth the Raven 'Nevermore'. Will I see my Chris, my Philip? Quoth the Raven 'Nevermore'.

Unable to lie still any longer, I crawl out of bed and make my way to the living room phone to dial Bill's number. A sleepy voice mumbles, "Hello?"

"Hello, Bill? This is Barbara. I'm sorry to wake you up but I have to talk to you about something." He stifles a yawn.

"Hello. I'm glad you called. I haven't heard from you lately and I've been worried. What's wrong?" He answers so graciously I can almost believe he enjoys being awakened at 2 A.M.

I curl up in the corner of the couch and pull the afghan around me. "Everything in my life is going fine, but I have this constant anxiety. I feel like something terrible is going to happen. It's the kind of feeling I had the week before Christopher died."

"That doesn't necessarily mean someone is going to die again." He's fully awake now and his voice comes through the receiver clearly.

"I'm not so sure. Remember when I told you that someone in our family has been dying every fourteen months? It happened three years in a row. At the end of January it will be fourteen months since Christopher died."

"Your feelings arise from the superstitious tendencies of human nature. When a few things happen in a sequence the mind tends to make a pattern of it, assumes that things will keep happening in just the same way."

"But it's not in my mind." I hear my voice coming out in a higher tone. "The fear comes over me when I'm not even thinking about it. And I'm not the only one in the family that's feeling it."

"That doesn't surprise me. Your family has been through years of trauma. You've picked up a pattern of anxiety, especially around these anniversary dates. Your subconscious sends messages, not only to your mind, but through your entire nervous system. That's what makes your body react."

My tensed throat and stomach muscles ease up a bit and I slump against the back of the couch. As a nurse I know his words are absolutely true. "You're probably right. I hope you're right." Something still doesn't feel right. "But Bill, how can I tell if I'm having that kind of anxiety, or if this is a true premonition? The kind I had before Christopher died?"

"There's no way to tell the difference. You'll have to live through this, and when nothing happens your fears will gradually dissipate." Dear Bill, as kind as he is, he never sugar-coats the truth. He adds gently, "I will be praying for you."

I surrender myself to the oppressive anxiety that permeates my space. I rest more, attempt to get involved in a fascinating novel, drink a little wine before dinner. I've learned not to push my body.

Mary calls one evening. "For the last few weeks I've been thinking a lot about Christopher. Do you realize that on February second it will be exactly fourteen months since he died? I don't want you calling me and telling me someone else has died."

Her last sentence trails up on the end making it sound like a question.

"We've got the fourteen month syndrome here too, especially Cathy and Peggy and I." I tell her about Bill's reassurance that it's just a superstitious pattern we've picked up because of our sequence of past tragedies. "Try not to worry about it. Everything's going to be okay." I try hard to make my voice sound convincing.

January 31st, early in the morning, Uncle Ray calls from the convalescent home to tell me Aunt Leone died in her sleep during the night. Tacky as it may be, when I receive this message, my instinct for self preservation causes me to breathe a sigh of relief. I know this is the fourteenth month blow we've been expecting and it's not as bad as I'd feared. I have loved Auntie since my childhood's first recollection of her, but she was old, suffering for years from severe arthritic spasms, and lately having hallucinations. "I'm ready to go," she kept telling me. "They keep us old people alive too long with their treatments and medicines. Life gets too hard when you're old."

After telling Harry, my first phone call is to our Eastside house. Peggy answers. "Uncle Ray just called." Before she has time to panic I say, "Aunt Leone died in her sleep last night." Her initial reaction is one of shock and sadness, then I hear no sound but her soft breathing coming through our connection. "Peggy?"

"Do you realize," she says finally, "that in two

days it would have been exactly fourteen months since Christopher died?"

"Yes. I've been counting too. We haven't broken the cycle yet, but at least this blow isn't as horrible as the others. Auntie has been praying to die for the last two years."

Her sigh makes a soft puffing sound in my ear. "I know she has. But I can't help wishing it wouldn't have happened right now."

"I have a feeling about this." For some reason, the news of Leone's death has lessened my fears of impending disaster. "I don't think our lives will be so bad anymore. Our troubles are winding down."

"Maybe."

"Anyway, I'll keep you posted on the funeral arrangements. Uncle's taking care of everything. Will you pass the news on to Cathy?" She promises to tell Cathy right away.

Aunt Leone was close to all of the children. They'll want to know. Carefully, I plan my strategy for informing them. It will be easy to tell Mike. He didn't buy into our fourteen month phobia. Peter is realistic also, not given to superstitious tendencies. But I can't possibly call Mary. She'll panic. I decide to tell Geri and ask her to call Mary. A phone call from Geri won't be as frightening for her. Judie's been worrying about another death, but she's strong. She's been through a lot. I decide to tell her myself.

As an afterthought I call Karen. She and Chris used to visit Aunt Leone. When Auntie moved into the nursing home she gave them many fine pieces of furniture for their new house. To my surprise, Karen already knew about her death. "My mother read it in the obituaries and called to tell me. I'm going to come to the wake tomorrow night. Are all of you going to be there?"

"Why . . yes," I stammer. Her willingness to share in this family gathering sets me aback. "At least all of us who live in Milwaukee."

"Good, I'll see you there." Her voice carries the brightness of enthusiasm I haven't heard since the old days before Christopher died.

"Well, good," I think after we hang up. "She's made a good recovery." I feel another layer of uneasiness peel away from my oppressive January mood.

We huddle in a small familial circle at the front of the nursing home's adjoining chapel, and look down into the casket at Aunt Leone. There's a feeling of peace about her. "She was suffering a lot," I say to the family. "I'm glad she's at rest." Heads bow in agreement.

Judie and Jardo have driven from Prairie Creek to be with us. "They've fixed her up to look so good," Judie comments. "This isn't the way I remember her."

"They made her look so young," Cathy says with a slow shake of her head. "I don't ever remember her looking like this."

"She never did look like this," says Mike bluntly. His artistic eye picks up the color-heightened hair, the wrinkle-free smoothness of the skin about her eyes and mouth, the unnatural fullness of her cheeks and jawline. "I think the morticians went a little overboard here."

I have to agree with him.

The chapel fills with Leone's old friends, those that are left, and with the new friends she made in the convalescent home. Uncle Ray leads us in a short prayer service. In his homily, he tells about her life of self sacrifice and the hours of loving care she gave him after he had his stroke fifteen years ago. We are all crying by the time he comes to his conclusion. "Her goodness was hidden in quiet, unassuming service to others."

We walk about visiting with the small clusters of mourners, and then gather together on one side of the chapel for a family visit. "I have something I want to tell all of you," Karen begins timidly. Her expression is a curious mixture of girlish delight and embarrassment. I wonder what's coming next. She holds out her left hand to display the glittering diamond on her third finger. Funny I didn't notice it earlier. "I've gotten engaged to Chet. You know, the Navy man that Chris and I always talked about. Remember, he's the one that often invited us to come over and swim in his pool?" Her words tumble out swiftly now that she's gotten started. I realize she's been holding this inside, wondering how and when to tell us.

"Chet has been so kind to me during this last year . . . helping me with the snow shoveling, and the yard work, all the hard jobs I had to do alone around the house. We've been spending a lot of time together. And I haven't always been good company.

He knows I still love Chris, that I always will. We talk about it. But he says he doesn't care, as long as I love him too."

Her face is glowing with a wide smile, her blue eyes shining with happiness. My reaction is one of joy. She has suffered so much, I'm glad she's found happiness again. We all express our pleasure in her new romance.

"He sounds wonderful, very supportive," says Judie. "Have you set a date?"

"He says he doesn't want to rush me. We'll probably wait till next September."

"That's very thoughtful of him. I'm happy for you, Karen," I say. Then I can't resist adding a teasing remark that comes to my mind. "But you know what this means, don't you?"

Karen's brows shoot up over her wide startled eyes. "What?"

"Once you get married, you have to turn in your OLIVE T-shirt." Laughter dispels the small bit of tension that's hanging about. On Christmas day, four years earlier, Philip gave everyone in the family white T-shirts with a big green pimento stuffed olive on the front.

"I'm trying to figure out how I can keep the name OLIVE along with my new married name," Karen says between chuckles.

"We'll have to talk to Chet about that," says Peggy.

Karen brings Chet to my birthday party in the middle of February and we all get to know him a little better. With his ready sense of humor and easy going manner, I feel we have added another friend to our family circle.

Sue is at our party along with Josh and Sarah. She's been dating again but not seriously enough to bring a new boyfriend to a family gathering. I can't help noticing she's begun curling her hair, wearing dressier clothes and makeup . . . and looking younger.

Three months later Josh graduates from eighth grade as the Salutatorian of his class. When he steps up to the podium to give his address his low voice startles me. Sometime during the last few years his voice changed without my noticing. When he joins us for refreshments later I see that he's taller than I am. Sue's eyes are red from crying. During Josh's speech she leaned over and whispered to me, "I wish Phil were here to see him." I cried too. The old pains cling with tenacious claws.

Shortly after that Karen calls to tell us the date she and Chet have set for the wedding. She talks excitedly about the plans they've made. She laughs when she tells me one of her sisters is pregnant and isn't sure if she'll be back in shape to fit into her bridesmaid gown. When the conversation slows down I insert, "By the way, what ever happened to Kenny's drunk driving conviction?"

"Oh, I guess I forgot to tell you. There was an initial hearing and his lawyer got the prosecuting attorney to drop the reckless driving and speeding charges, and press for the drunk driving charge only.

I don't know how this all came about, but it sounds like they'll be set for the actual trial sometime this summer."

"It's amazing how long this can get dragged out."

"I'm pretty disgusted with this whole justice system. I don't even like to think about it anymore. I'll call you, though, when I find out when the trial is going to be held."

"Good. We want to be there."

Instead of our usual family camping trip, we make plans for the entire family to travel to the East Coast for a week at the seashore along Cape Cod. We're ready for some big time fun.

Peter and Jill rent two houses on the inward curl of the cape, and I call car and bus rental companies to find a large van that will hold the dozen children that want to drive there. Those of us with spare cash make our plane reservations.

Just before we leave in August, I receive a letter from a person who identifies herself as Ken's parole officer. She requests that our family members contact her to discuss the charges and sentencing of the young man charged with Christopher's death. I call the number she has listed and hear her say, "I can't advise you what to think, but I want you to know that Ken hasn't been compliant while out on bail. He's been seen drinking, which was strictly forbidden, and also has been spotted driving after drinking in public."

"Driving and drinking! After what he did? Well

that changes the whole picture. I had thought some sort of community service and suspension of his driver's license . . but now? I'd hate to think of him out on the road driving like that, maybe killing again. I guess a prison term is the answer. What do you think this will mean in terms of his conviction?"

"It changes the situation. He's hired a new lawyer, he claims his old one didn't tell him he wasn't supposed to drink while out on bail. He keeps insisting that he has not driven a car after drinking, but we have a witness who will testify otherwise. We're scheduling another hearing on the issue of his 'bail jumping'."

"When is that going to be held?" She gives me the phone number of the prosecuting district attorney who can tell us the date. With my attention diverted to the Cape Cod trip, I put off calling and allow the matter to slip from my mind.

This is the first time in my life I've watched the tide come in, and then roll out again, leaving a half-mile of rippled sand scattered with seashells and tiny crabs and jellyfish. I find it fascinating. "Don't step on the jellyfish," Peter warns. "They'll sting your feet." The ocean water is surprisingly warm along the cape—shallow enough to be safe for the smaller children.

We haven't all been together since the Christmas after Christopher died a year and a half ago. In spite of the fun, at times I need to go off by myself and grieve that Philip and Chris aren't here. Mostly we laugh and play together or take side trips to explore our new environment.

Mary tells us about the college courses she's signed up for, which in two years will complete her degree in working with the learning disabled. "I had to get out of that bank job. It was too boring." she tells us one evening sitting around the dinner table. "I felt like my life was going nowhere. Now I'm enthused about my future. I guess I've wanted to do something like this all along; just didn't realize it."

Peggy invites everyone to her graduation in December. She'll have her Master's in Social Welfare. "What a relief! "I've been going to school for twenty years . . . counting kindergarten."

"You're so lucky, Peggy," says Cathy becoming serious. "I've just signed up for a semester at the university. I'm going back for a degree in psychology. I want to be a clinical psychologist. I've been seeing so many people messing up their lives, and I want to know why. I want to help them. It will help me too. Maybe some day I'll open my own clinic—make serious headway helping people untangle their lives."

⫸ 22 ⫷

Final Sentence

Mike, Cathy, Peggy and I wait impatiently in the foyer of the County Court House. There's some delay in starting the proceedings. "So what's new?" I say. "Two years and two months since Christopher's death, and our justice system has just now gotten around to sentencing Kenny." Last month he was convicted of homicide by intoxicated use of a motor vehicle and bail jumping.

We huddle in one corner of the foyer, making occasional trips to the water cooler or restroom. Near the double doors leading to the courtroom another group is gathering. They're clustered closely together looking as uneasy as we are feeling. We look at them stealthily, not wishing to be rude and stare. Now and then I catch one of them casting a quick glance toward us.

I've never seen Kenny before but I pick him out of the group at once. He's just the way Karen described him . . . a young black male, tall and well built, clean shaven, a pleasing appearance but with a jaw line a little weak to be considered truly handsome. He's a classy dresser—dark suit, white shirt and tie, long black topcoat. A professional image.

I point him out to the children and they agree he must be the one. We talk stealthily about how nervous Kenny must be right now. We comment about the large group of friends accompanying him. As we stand there I begin to sense a growing desire to speak with him. I'm not sure why, or what I would say. I go over a few opening lines in my head. "Hello. I'm Christopher's mother. You must be Kenny." Karen always called him Kenny. I noticed the parole officer called him Ken. I wonder which he would prefer. Then what would he say? Would he extend his hand and say he's pleased to meet me? Or would he draw back looking aloof and angry?

The longer we stand and wait the stronger my impulse grows. Finally I say to Cathy (Mike and Peggy have left for the washrooms), "I want to say hello to Kenny." My voice trails up at the end as though I'm asking for permission. I check for the reaction on her face.

No surprise registers there. "I'd like to speak to him too," she admits, "but I'd feel kind of stupid walking up and breaking into their circle."

"I wonder if they feel hostile toward us? You know, Chris vs. Kenny?"

"They might."

When Mike and Peggy return we tell them what we've been talking about. "Do you think I should just go over and introduce myself?"

"Sure, Mom," says Peggy. "I don't think I could, but if that's what you want to do, go ahead."

"What could it hurt?" adds Mike.

Still I hang back feeling awkward. Kenny's distress begins reaching out to me from across the lobby. The outcome of this hour will change years of his life. "This isn't right," I say at last. "Us standing here and *them* over there. I'm going over and introduce myself."

"Go for it Mom." Cathy gives me an encouraging smile.

I begin crossing the ten-foot marble span that separates us. I see Ken's friends eye me apprehensively, then give him a nudge. He turns in my direction. There is no hostility in his eyes. His expression is warm and friendly. He breaks away from his group and strides towards me extending his hand as he approaches.

"Hello, I'm Ken. You must be Chris's mother. I've been wanting to meet you." He gives me a moment to return his introduction then goes on talking at length about how he wanted to come to Chris's funeral; how much he wanted to talk to us about what had happened; how badly he felt about the whole thing, all the while continuing to shake my hand. "They wouldn't let me get in touch with any of you. The lawyers don't allow any communication between the parties of the defense and those of the prosecution."

I have to tilt my head back to talk to him. He's even taller close up. "We thought it might be something like that. I suppose they don't want anyone to say something that might be used as evidence."

"Yes. But I've been wanting you to know how sorry I am." His voice sounds sincere, his eyes start glinting with unshed tears. "Chris was a good friend to me. I only knew him for six months, but we hit it off right from the start. He was a wonderful person."

"Yes, we thought so too. I want you to know that I don't feel any anger towards you. I know you didn't intend to hurt Chris. It was just a foolish mistake. One that turned out very badly."

Ken and I are standing alone halfway between the two opposing groups. Cathy, Peggy, and Mike start walking our way. "I want you to meet Chris's brother and sisters." I make the introductions. Ken repeats to them how sad he feels about all that has happened, and how much he's been wanting to meet them. They shake hands all around.

"We're not mad at you," Cathy says. "We know it was just a crazy accident. Chris did some pretty crazy things himself." Peggy nods in agreement. Mike's body language tells me he hasn't quite decided.

The courtroom door opens and the guard motions for us to come in. Ken excuses himself and rejoins his support group. We follow, parting from the other group halfway up the center aisle, Ken's followers sliding into benches on the right behind the defense attorney, while we edge into seats behind the prosecutor on the left. Why separate sides? Do the opposing groups tend to fight with each other? I don't know. It just feels like the right thing to do;

Like being in church and taking his and her sides at a wedding.

The judge speaks first explaining the nature of the proceedings, then goes on to fill us in on the background of the accident and conviction. Next Ken's lawyer makes a forty-five minute long plea for leniency, citing Ken's family and their stability in the community; Ken's fine scholastic accomplishments which have culminated in a professional career in computer technology. He reads sections of letters from Ken's friends and co-workers testifying to his fine character. We squirm on our hard benches and keep looking at our watches.

Next the prosecuting attorney expounds on the difficulty Ken has had in the past with alcohol, his troubled driving record, his unsatisfactory behavior while out on bail. He quotes the parole officer's testimony, written police records, details of past misbehaviors, and any other evidence he can quote testifying to Ken's unreliability.

When he finally returns to his seat, the judge starts recapping the whole scenario before passing sentence. He admits that he has received many letters from the community requesting leniency for Ken. "But Christopher was also very much loved by those who knew him. I have received letters from his family, and to their credit, they are not screaming for Ken's blood. They have expressed compassion for his plight and have requested leniency in his sentencing." He concludes that if Ken had not broken his bail contract by drinking and also driving after drinking he would have imposed a lighter sentence. "As it is, I feel compelled to impose the maximum sentence allowed by law."

Ken rises to hear his sentence. Silence suspends all court room bustle. "Three years in prison for the original charge, plus three years in prison for 'bail jumping', the second three years to be served concurrently with the first, followed by one year probation and one hundred hours of community service. The community service is to be in the nature of appearances at schools and youth organizations testifying to the dangers of drinking and driving." The judge goes on to say Ken will be eligible for parole in not less than nine months nor more than two years. Mike whispers to us that a three year sentence is never more than two years plus a year of parole.

Ken reads a final speech he has prepared. He begins to cry and has a hard time completing it. He tells us how sorry he is for taking Christopher from us and causing us so much pain. We cry with him. When the judge dismisses us, Mike crosses the aisle to speak to Ken. We have filed out into the lobby before Mike rejoins us. "I wanted to wish him 'good luck'," he explains. The anger in Mike's heart has been washed away by Ken's tears.

An attractive red-haired young woman approaches Mike. "I know you are Christopher's brother. You look just like him." Mike nods in agreement and shakes the hand she offers him. "I met Chris for the first time the night before he died. We were both from big families so we spent about an hour comparing notes about life with siblings. . .

how we used to fight about who got to sleep on the top bunk, stuff like that. We had so much in common we felt like old buddies. I couldn't believe it in the morning when I found out he was dead." She turns and introduces herself to all of us. "I'm so glad I got to meet you."

"It's good to meet you," says Mike and we all agree. "Yeh, Chris was a pretty neat guy. Didn't come much better."

"I could tell, just meeting him once. I'm terribly sorry this happened to him." She says goodbye and hurries out the door to join her friends.

We fill the rest of the family in on the day's proceedings. We talk about how the justice system dehumanizes people, prevents them from communicating, pits them against each other. I call Karen and tell her what happened at the sentencing. She tells me, "That day I went to Ken's trial and saw how sad we was, my feelings about him changed too. I felt sorry for him." Like Mike, Karen's anger against Ken has drained away.

What followed next changed the hearts of Peter, Jardo, and the rest of those who were hanging on to their anger.

In February a letter arrives from Ken, the return address . . . a Wisconsin prison:

> "Let me begin by saying that I agree
> with the Assistant District Attorney when he
> said, 'Christopher's light shown brightly' and
> that 'he was loved by those who knew him.'
> It saddens me more than anyone could know

that Chris is not here today. I played a role in that . . and will have to live with that knowledge for the rest of my life. The three years in prison . . my punishment, pales in comparison to the personal and emotional pain that I have. When I do get out of prison I will endeavor to become an outstanding citizen once again and try to deter people from causing the pain that I have. If there is anything I can say or do that would help, please let me know. I will be forever in your debt. I regret that I did not meet you until my sentencing. You are beautiful people. God bless you."

The letter gets passed through the family and we puzzle over what Ken could possibly do that would help us. Karen wonders what Chris talked about that last night. The children agree that it would be consoling to know about Chris's thoughts and actions during those last hours. I send the request off to Ken. He replies early in March.

"It comes as no great surprise to me that you would find many ways to remember Chris - I will never forget him for the rest of my days. In the few months that I knew him I think it is safe to say that we thought of each other as friends. On that unfortunate night, Chris and I talked mainly of work, we were joined by another friend, a new employee so the crux of our conversation was 'small talk'."

Of course. To Chris it seemed like any other night out. I stop to consider how few people get to do and say something profound during their final hours. . . and how many never get to say 'goodbye'.

In Ken's next letter he expresses loneliness at being cut off from family and friends. He tells us he's tutoring other prisoners in math, spelling, and computer. He talks about the AA meetings he attends, and the Bible study once a week. I tell the family about his letter and we agree that prison sounds like a wholesome and productive place. We exchange letters about once a month and on a whim I ask him to describe his surroundings and some of his fellow prisoners. His reply is not what I expected.

His letter comes in July just as we're packing to leave on our annual family camping trip to Point Beach. When all the family has settled into camp and we've gathered around the campfire, I pass Ken's letter around to those who want to read it:

> "I did take some time to think on your question about prison. I was going to 'sugar-coat' my experience in the Corrections Department so as not to worry anyone. (My family receives the 'I'm fine, it's not bad spiel). You noticed that I was transferred to a different institution during my first month. I received a serious threat to my life in the

first place. I am by no means a small person, but there is not much you can do against two or three assailants.

"... Most of the inmates in this new facility are under twenty-two years of age and don't care about too much. From what I have seen of it the prison population is about forty percent black, forty percent white, and twenty percent other (Hispanic, Oriental, etc.). I have never seen such racial hatred in all my life. The bathroom walls have to be washed daily because of racial slurs. There have been five racial fights since I've been here and numerous yelling and shoving matches. In one instance a youth came forward because he had had enough of the 'initiation rites' that the Aryan Nation Chapter members put him through. He showed administration where the gang kept their weapons and homemade tattoo gun. They transferred him immediately to protective custody and then transferred one gang leader to a different institution."

"I don't get involved with any of that gang or racial stuff. That's one reason the administration wants to keep me in this institution. They think I have a calming influence on the Black and Hispanic youths. I think a better word for it is respect. They all (blacks, whites, etc,) respect my wishes. I told the blacks I don't want to hear any racial remarks or plots and I told the white guys the same thing. What frightens me is that I am going to have a confrontation with an inmate sooner or later.

"There is an inmate here who was one of the organizers of the Aryan Nation Chapter here. He has channeled his energies into satanic worship now. He has a hard core group of about six guys who pray to satan and denounce the Lord with vulgarities. Administration tried to stop them from receiving library books through the mail on satanic worship, demonology, witchcraft, etc., but a lawsuit was threatened for censorship and the officials have backed off. This kind of stuff is just as bad, if not worse than the racial stuff that goes on here.

"One thing I can't stomach is that the guards here are in a feud with administration and we inmates are caught in the middle. A close knit group of three men have worked here as guards for quite some time and the administration is currently trying to fire one of them. The other two are siding with him, and to backlog administration they are issuing conduct reports to inmates for minor offenses (dust under bed, missing breakfast, etc.). That's bad for us because the Parole Board looks at your file and doesn't look favorably on an inmate with conduct reports in his file. That just touches the surface with the staff here.

"One of the older inmates told me a story

of how two large black men pinned him down and patted him down because they thought he was a cop checking for drugs! A little side note: If you want drugs or alcohol you can get it; the corrections system does random urinalysis, but I've been in six months and I've only received one. I don't do drugs and my drinking days are over.

"Last, but certainly not least, there is homosexuality here. Not all of it is with mutual consent. I have not heard of anyone being raped here but they recently transferred an inmate back to maximum security because he had raped someone at a different institution, and he told another inmate here that he was going to rape him as soon as he got the chance. I have a high suspicion that one of the support staff is having sexual relations with the younger kids here. I told staff about it because I don't want him taking advantage of these troubled youths. You have to be careful though, because the only thing all inmates hate is a 'snitch'.

"That's what prison life is like from what little I have seen of it. I have heard horror stories from some of the other inmates who have been at a maximum security institution. I try to keep busy and use my time constructively, as best I can, trying to better myself and, if possible, those around me. God Bless!!"

"He's paying a terrible price for what he did to Chris," Harry shakes his head. Mike, Jardo, and Peter are not too surprised by this letter. It's mostly us women who are distressed by this inside look at prison life. I've seen these corrupt prison scenes in movies and on TV but always assumed they were mostly products of the screenwriter's imagination. I begin incorporating Ken's safety into my daily prayers. To my relief he's transferred to a saner minimum security prison for intensive alcoholic counseling in October.

We don't hear from Ken until February. The letter has a normal street address on it. He was released from prison before Christmas having served eleven months of his three year prison term. Most of us are relieved to hear he's back at home, but his letter tells us his troubles aren't over:

"I still have two years of parole followed by three years of probation to complete. It's is more difficult than I thought it would be to readjust back into mainstream society. I have sent my resume out to many firms; however, when I go to the interview and tell them that I am a convicted felon I seem to always get a boilerplate rejection letter indicating that someone else is more qualified.

I am currently going to alcohol outpatient treatment, after having completed the eight week inpatient program in prison. It was helpful . . . I only wish that I would have gone many years ago. I am very sorry for all the pain and suffering that I caused you and your family. Not a day goes by that I don't think about my accident. I am constantly reminded of it. Even though I haven't written for a while I think of you fondly and often. God bless you. Ken"

My next letter to Ken is returned unopened. He moved and left no forwarding address.

Like Ken, tragedy has forced many of us to live with a new set of circumstances and play by a new set of rules. With purified eyes we see farther horizons, and must stretch our skills to reach them. I get serious about writing to the point of studying rules of grammar and elements of style. Writing workshops lure me on to consider publishing, particularly the ultimate workshop for authors and wannabe's, the Santa Barbara Writers' Conference.

Sarah, now in high school, takes a class in journalism. Sue sends us a copy of her poem which was published in her school newspaper:

Daddy's Little Girl

"What I would give to be able to share
The good times and the bad,
Or just have someone to be there
Through times that make me sad.

What I would give to have a smile
On my face while someone would
Walk me down the aisle
To give me away like he should.

What I would give to share with you
An ice cream cone with one big swirl.
What I would give to be able to do
The things that make me Daddy's little girl."

Mike secures his Master of Fine Arts degree and begins teaching at the university. He completes one more art project overtly directed to the healing of his grief . . . and ours. He presents the family with a life-sized oil portrait of Christopher, which he has painted from photographs and from memory. Chris, wearing his T-shirt and jeans, walks toward us through a filmy luminous background with his hand extended palm upward in greeting. His smile is radiant, his eyes glow with joy and tenderness. I hang the picture at the top of the second floor landing so it's easily seen from both the second and first floor levels. Sometimes when we're passing Christopher's portrait we reach out and touch his hand. It comforts us daily.

⫸ Epilogue ⫷

Fourteen years have passed since Philip died. I've written four books and have been invited to lecture and take part in bereavement groups. Tonight I'm speaking to a gathering of the newly bereaved telling them the good news: "You will be done grieving some day and you will be happy again." I never omit the bad news. "It's a mountainous journey of ups and downs that takes a very long time. Longer than I ever imagined. Longer than any of us want or expect."

When I arrive at this meeting I discover it's the same group Sue, Josh, and Sarah attended to seek help in their grieving. The session leader is the same one that guided Sue through healing and recovery. Without bereavement groups like this, with their dedicated leaders, and without skilled and compassionate counselors and therapists for individual guidance, we would have far fewer emotionally stable individuals in our midst. I urge all of you whose loved ones were a tragic news flash on the 6 o'clock report, and all of you passersby who carry about a hidden tragedy, to participate in every healing method available to you.

If, like Ken, you were the one whose actions caused the trauma, take heart. Life can be good again. Ignore the critics and the grumblers and open yourself to the healing and peace waiting for you. We all stumble and fall on this journey. We all need a helping hand to rise again and walk toward tomorrow's hope.

No, your life will never be the same; you will be changed forever. What will astonish you is how grief can transform you into a fully alive human being. This radical transformation was revealed to one of my support group members in a dream he had near the end of his healing process. This is the dream he shared with us:

"I found myself walking through a dense woods when my path was suddenly obstructed by a large pond. The water looked dark and deep but, in spite of my fear, I walked straight into it. For a time I was completely submerged, but I forced myself to keep walking and at last I emerged on the opposite bank, dripping with water, but unharmed."

The dream stayed with me on awakening and I felt calm and reassured. I had walked through the dark waters of grief, accepted my loss, and survived. The sensation of being drenched when I emerged let me know that I could never be the same person I was before, because my walk through grief had profoundly changed my beliefs, attitudes, and life goals."

My own grief has altered what I used to call 'my life'. I was an embryo when I began grieving. I'm expanding to fill the world, even beginning to fill the heavens where Phil and Chris and my Mom and Dad are companying with God. In each expansion He is ahead of me, smiling, surprising, delighting to show me the new vistas with the promise of more to come.

The Olive Tree
Barbara and Harry Olive

<u>Children</u> (oldest to youngest)	<u>Grandchildren</u>	<u>Residence</u>
Judie (Engineering) married Jardo (Postmaster)	Theresa Jessica Michelle	Prairie Creek
Philip (deceased) married Sue (Social Work)	Josh Sarah	Erin
Peter (Engineering) married Jill (Preschool Teacher)	Eddie Molly Jeffrey	Boston
Mike (Artist) married Janel (Artist)	Matthew	Milwaukee
Mary (Speech Therapist) married Mike (Warehouse Mngr.)	Carli	Brookston
Christopher (deceased) married Karen (Insurance)		Milwaukee
Geri (Nurse)		Milwaukee
Cathy (Respiratory Therapist)		Milwaukee
Peggy (Social Work)		Milwaukee